I AM JEREMIAH

By the same author:
I am Joseph

I am Jeremiah

(Don't Laugh)

ALAN PAIN

KINGSWAY PUBLICATIONS

EASTBOURNE

Biblical quotations are from the
New International Version © 1973, 1978, 1984
by the International Bible Society.
Anglicisation © 1979, 1984 by Hodder and Stoughton Ltd

Front cover illustration by Taffy Davies
Illustrations by Sue Lea

British Library Cataloguing in Publication Data

Pain, Alan
I am Jeremiah.
1. Bible. O.T. Characters. Jeremiah
I. Title
224'.20924

ISBN 0-86065-722-1

Printed in Great Britain for
KINGSWAY PUBLICATIONS LTD
1 St Anne's Road, Eastbourne, E. Sussex BN21 3UN by
BPCC Hazell Books, Aylesbury, Bucks, England
Member of BPCC Ltd.
Typeset by Nuprint Ltd, Harpenden, Herts AL5 4SE.

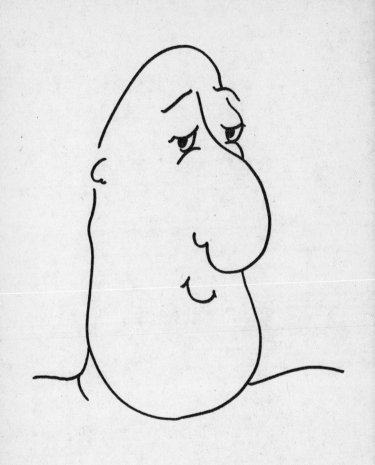

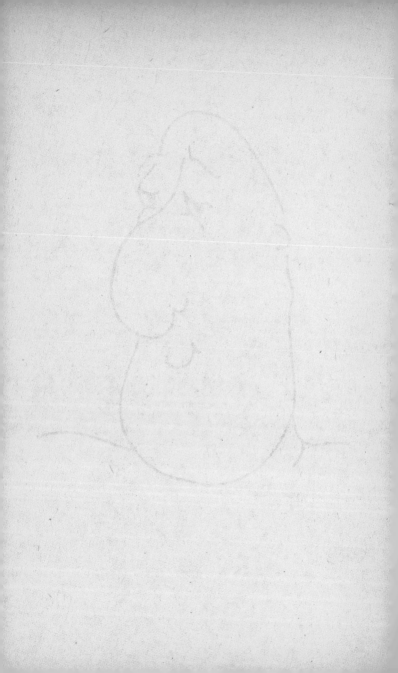

To my wife Lyn,
a very special partner,
whose persistence in wholefoods
has taught me the difference between good figs—
and bad (Jeremiah 24:1–4).

Contents

Contents

Introduction

Jeremiah is too good to miss, but few of us know him at all, and even fewer know him well. This is an attempt to introduce Jeremiah, using the licence of an imaginary autobiography to allow him to describe a life of calamity, embarrassment and spiritual struggle.

Jeremiah was not a social reformer, but he wanted to reform the social order. He was not a predicter of the future, but he prophesied with confidence of events to come. He was a man of God who lived in the seventh and sixth centuries BC, called into a unique mission which he reluctantly accepted of preparing Israel for an exile in Babylon she expected to avoid. The nation resented Jeremiah's view that the exile was inevitable as God's judgement on a bunch of rebels, and they resisted his plea for them to settle down in Babylon for a long stay.

Jeremiah began to prophesy around the year 627 BC, and his public ministry lasted more than forty years. He saw the first exile in 597, and the second disastrous deportation in 586 which followed Zedekiah's suicidal revolt and Nebuchadnezzar's long punitive siege of Jerusalem which ended in the fall of the city, the destruction of the Temple and the further movement of significant people to

Babylon. The biblical record of these events is found in 2 Kings 24–25, to which the book of Jeremiah adds vivid and compelling details of the prophet's own life.

I have resisted the temptation of pride to pepper the book with scholarly references and quotations, despite my forlorn desire for academic respectability. Those who read this book are unlikely to read the scholars who will, not unreasonably, pass by on the other side. But I have enjoyed myself.

You can use this treatment of Jeremiah for personal reading, home-group studies, preaching preparation and exams, provided you separate imagination from interpretation. Some 'A' level teaching has stirred in me the desire to encourage students into a closer private reading of Jeremiah, and the idea for this book came from working with them, including my two daughters. I have valued their encouragement.

A number of outstanding books on the life and teaching of Jeremiah have helped me, notably J Skinner's *Prophecy and Religion*, although it was published nearly seventy years ago. At times it's amusing to note how much recent writers, myself included, have absorbed Skinner's work!

But most of all I have benefited from running round Sutton Park thinking about this remarkable man who had so little intention of being funny. Anyone who has heard an idiot jogger burst into sudden laughter may now know the secret: I was thinking about Jeremiah. I comfort myself that he's nothing like me, but sometimes I'm not so sure. However, I like him, and I hope you will.

I

My Call

I am Jeremiah the Prophet. You would never have heard of me if I had had my way, but it's too late now to turn back the clock. I was dragged unwillingly from the obscurity I wanted to keep into the renown I always shunned. I spent years creeping backstage, but the spotlight followed me 'with unhurrying chase and unperturbed pace' (Francis Thompson, *Hound of Heaven*). By now I am proverbial to you through the saying, 'He's a right Jeremiah.' That means a depressing and pessimistic person who will be the wet blanket at every party. Perhaps you're right though, any publicity is good publicity and even an unfavourable proverb in your honour is its own backhanded compliment.

I am not a prophet by choice but by the irresistible will of God. I follow in a marvellous succession of men who, although very different from each other, have been the right men in the right place at the right time—and God has used them. We have not been professional prophets; prophecy has not run in our families and our vindication appears fearfully flimsy at times, but we believe God has called us. False prophets can claim their visions and their ecstasies, but they have not been called, and I have

13

learned how to denounce them: 'I have not sent them or appointed them or spoken to them. They are prophesying to you false visions, divinations, idolatries and the delusions of their own minds' (Jer 14:14). You cannot choose to be a prophet and there are no volunteers; you simply come when God calls you.

Take Amos for example. A real black-and-white man was Amos. He saw things starkly and they were either right or wrong; there was no middle course. Amos made friends and Amos made enemies, and you had to be for him or against him, for that's how he was towards you. Amos was the first of our prophets to give his name to written prophecy. He was gripped and compelled by his call and he went forward in untroubled obedience. God laid on him an inescapable constraint which he made no apparent attempt to avoid. That was the sole authentication of Amos' prophecy and it was ample for him. He pictured it dramatically in terms of cause and effect. A lion does not snarl from the bush unless it has seized its prey. Two people do not walk together in the desert unless they have made arrangements to meet. A bird does not writhe in the trap unless the snare has been set for it. So a man does not prophesy unless God has called him (see Amos 3:1–8). It was that logical for Amos. He was ready and waiting when Amaziah challenged him: 'Get out, you seer! Go back to the land of Judah' (Amos 7:12). (You and I would say, 'Why don't you go back where you came from?') Amaziah was the resident priest at the Bethel shrine. He knew Amos was no more than a shepherd who supplemented his income by looking after sycamore figtrees—the first moonlighter. He wanted Amos to stay that way, for he resented this southerner from Judah who interfered in the northern kingdom of Israel with ruthless denunciations which pointed out the close connections between the social and religious righteousness of the nation.

Amos' uncompromising reply to Amaziah was brief

and to the point: 'The Lord took me from tending the flock and said to me, "Go prophesy to my people Israel." Now then, hear the word of the Lord' (Amos 7:15–16). Amos knew his call, and that made him sure of everything else. I wish I had found such confidence infectious.

Hosea came next, almost contemporary with Amos. If you compare Hosea with Amos you won't find a better example of chalk and cheese. Hosea saw the black and white which Amos saw, but his emotional upheavals painted in all sorts of shades between the black and white. The breakdown of his marriage threw him into turmoil. His unfaithful wife, Gomer, constantly broke his heart, forcing him to see the anguish in the heart of God who was confronted by his adulterous people, Israel. His obedience to his summons was costly. The pressure upon him was a pressure to act as well as to speak, and that became his call to be a prophet. It came from God and laid a mighty constraint upon him. Through the tragedy of his home, Hosea received his call: 'Go, take to yourself an adulterous wife and children of unfaithfulness, because the land is guilty of the vilest adultery in departing from the Lord' (Hos 1:2). Amos revealed so little of himself and Hosea so much, but both were called by God.

I don't understand Isaiah, not least because he controlled his feelings in a way which I could neither imitate nor fathom, but how I admire him! God called him, and he came willingly and eagerly when I would have been speeding away in the opposite direction. ' "Whom shall I send? And who will go for us?" And I said, "Here am I. Send me!" ' (Is 6:8). In that tense and awesome moment of Temple worship, which was majestic with the presence of God, Isaiah became a prophet. His lips were now *clean*, his life was now *commissioned* and his message now had its *content*. (See Isaiah 6:5–10—preachers, you are welcome to these sermon headings.) Isaiah pleaded for national repentance. He expected only a dispirited remnant to survive inevitable catastrophe. He knew the nation was suffering from a heart incurably hardened, but he went on. Isaiah persisted calm and resolute for over forty years in his vain battle to persuade the people to repent. He knew his warning of terrible judgement would pass unheeded. I would not have volunteered for that. But Isaiah stuck to his guns because he had been called by God.

Ezekiel is younger than I am, but what a mystery he is! I'd been a prophet for more than thirty years when he began. I've felt misunderstood myself at times, but that's nothing compared with Ezekiel. He saw the Lord sitting on his heavenly throne, and in a vision that was strange and wonderful he was given a scroll to eat. 'Son of man, eat what is before you, eat this scroll; then go and speak to the house of Israel' (Ezek 3:1). You can mock Ezekiel and you can be confused by him, but he knew he was called by God.

Then there was Jeremiah. I came kicking and scream-ing. I began unwillingly and I continued reluctantly. My call closed in on me, confining me as if in a cell locked firmly from the outside. I never did find the exit. In my call to be a prophet I heard words which were both wonderful and shattering: 'Before I formed you in the womb I knew you, before you were born I set you apart; I appointed you as a prophet to the nations' (Jer 1:5). It was a mind-boggling possibility that God was setting before me. At any other time I would have been happy even to dream of a message like that, but it's the last thing you want to hear when you're running away. The trouble is that ever since that moment I've increasingly realised that what I heard is true. I see a thread, strong and unbroken, holding together the whole of my life and working through it from the beginning. I did the only thing I could think of—I hid behind my youth. 'Ah, Sovereign Lord... I do not know how to speak; I am only a child' (Jer 1:6). As if he hadn't heard me he pursued me. You'd have thought I was Jonah.

I was not unsure about my call; far from it. I was not

confused. God wanted me to speak as a prophet. Whenever there is a national crisis God calls up his man. I was young, but even I could grasp the unalterable movement of events which was pointing to the break-up of Judah, the end of Jerusalem, the ruin of the Temple and the exile of judgement. I knew exactly what our people needed and I hoped it wasn't Jeremiah. How then do you explain your call, especially to those who want to silence you? How can you be certain for yourself that you have been called?

* The circumstances at the time allow you no way out. All the doors are shutting except one which is ajar and threatening to swing wide open.
* There is no peace of mind in any alternative path, even though you tell yourself that you're settled and relaxed in what you're doing, with no thought of a change.
* Every day your life looks more like a jig-saw puzzle which doesn't fit until you yield to the spiritual pressure upon you.
* You've played at God's will before, but this is clearly final; all the discussions are finished and now it's time for action.
* A strange, eerie awareness is with you, and it grins from every hoarding, 'You are being called.'

Finally, you agree. You belong to God and your life has already been vowed to him. You are like a servant who is offered his freedom, but when it comes to it he doesn't want to be anywhere else. When I claimed, brazenly but hurt, that the Lord had enticed me and overpowered me—'You deceived me, and I was deceived; you overpowered me and prevailed' (Jer 20:7), I was protesting at his compelling purpose and my total inability to offer lasting resistance. I followed; slowly, reluctantly, always wanting the exit which was never there.

I wasn't short of promises and I had pictures as well. That's more than enough for most people who would jump at full-time service if they had matching words and

pictures. But I'm the kind of man who always reads the small print. I want more than promises; I want to know what I'm being promised. I have enough Jewish blood in me to ask, 'What's the cost?' The pictures were fair enough, and I'll tell you more about them later. They captured God's word for me in a memorable way, and I can assure you now that the picture which pointed to God watching over his word, awake and alert, came to me regularly through the blossom of the almond tree (Jer 1:11–12). I drew vital encouragement from it many times. Equally, my entire message was painted on a canvas whose backcloth was the danger from the North which I saw through a boiling pot, tilting from that direction (Jer 1:13–14).

But what about the promises? I was to uproot and tear down nations and kingdoms. I was to destroy and over-throw. The people would fight against me, but I was not to be terrified (Jer 1:10, 17–19). Big deal! I was still a petrified teenager, covered in spots and pimples, with mere fluff on my chin. The Lord was unmoved by my protests, as usual. The pattern of my life was set in these promises and they were not what a young man who is determined to have a quiet life wants to hear. Opposition, hostility and total rejection; they were all heading in my direction, and I was expected to choose this way for myself. I thought it was a needless form of suicide. I was to be 'a fortified city, an iron pillar and a bronze wall' (Jer 1:18). I'd rather have been a normal teenager. I was told not to marry and to keep away from family life: 'You must not marry and have sons or daughters in this place' (Jer 16:2). I was to avoid family funerals and family parties. This was a fabulous release in most cases, but have you tried missing Granny's funeral when everyone thought you should be there, and then sending your excuse 'God told me to stop away. And I won't be at Granddad's either!'?

No, I wanted the support and companionship of relatives; I didn't want them at my throat. I've read the Proverbs as well as you have, 'Better to live in a desert than with a quarrelsome and ill-tempered wife'; 'A quarrelsome wife is like a constant dripping on a rainy day' (Prov 21:19; 27:15). The difficulty is that I don't believe these are the only options for marriage, and where I live we don't have rainy days.

I should have learned my lesson from our history. Moses tried every trick in the book to evade the call of God. He ducked and weaved, but to no avail (Ex 3:1— 4:13). Why should I fare any better? Samuel, a young boy, merely wanted a good night's sleep so that he could play more the next day, but God woke him up several nights running. What disturbed nights for poor old Eli (1 Sam 3). That's what you can expect if God is after you. Yes, I know you think it's a privilege to be chosen from the time before your conception, but it's also frightening.

There is a testimony in all this. It is definitely not your usual smiling, joyful testimony of victory because my testimonies all force themselves through gritted teeth. I have looked at faces and refused to be daunted. My fears have been lifted and God has been with me. He has never failed me when I've genuinely attempted what he wanted me to do. This testimony comes not in radiant calm but in desperate honesty. Nothing in my life has been radiant or calm; read on and you'll see for yourself.

2

My Early Life and Times

I wonder if the name Anathoth means anything to you? In fact, it's the place where I was born and grew up. Even now it remains a welcome retreat, despite the active hostility towards me of some local people and the angry rejection of my family. 'This is what the Lord says about the men of Anathoth who are seeking your life and saying, "Do not prophesy in the name of the Lord or you will die by our hands" ' (Jer 11:21). 'Your brothers, your own family—even they have betrayed you' (Jer 12:6).

Anathoth is an undiscovered jewel which has so far escaped the commercialisation which tourists inevitably provoke. It is hardly more than an hour's walk from Jerusalem and it provides everything you could want for a 'get away from it all' few days. I only hope no one will erect shrines on every scenic site. The views all around are breathtaking, and the wild and lonely landscape hushes you into silent wonder. Even children catch the mood and are quiet. When you approach Anathoth from Jerusalem, you'll see it first from the northern end of the Olivet range of hills. It lies on a hillside and is surrounded by hills where fig trees grow. On arrival you can look out to the North and the mountains of Israel are in front of you.

Turn to the East and you'll be confronted by the desolate hills towards the Jordan valley. Jerusalem itself lies to the South, and its rich history gives an exciting and comprehensive perspective to the view. At a very young age I was hooked on the fascinating natural world around my home.

My own passion is bird-watching. Migratory birds in particular have caught my imagination by their incredible instincts of timing and direction. If only some of our Temple-goers would imitate their faultless punctuality! I've spent hours thinking about these birds, and it has struck me that all sorts of practical applications can be drawn from them to challenge the spiritual life of our nation. 'Even the stork in the sky knows her appointed seasons, and the dove, the swift and the thrush observe the time of their migration. But my people do not know the requirements of the Lord' (Jer 8:7; cf 12:9; 17:11). These birds only have their natural instincts, but they respond swiftly to them. We have our minds and our faith which allow us to know God, but our response is wayward and rebellious. I found the comparison stark and chastening, and I called on the people to listen to me.

I have travelled widely on my bird-watching trips and I well remember my visits to the mountains of Lebanon. The peaks there are always covered with snow and I've gazed at them for hours as I've climbed in search of nests and other traces of the birds I've come to see. These snow covered heights have spoken to me again and again of the absolute faithfulness of God, to which his people make a dismissive and contemptuous response. 'Does the snow of Lebanon ever vanish from its rocky slopes? Do its cool waters from distant sources ever cease to flow? Yet my people have forgotten me' (Jer 18:14–15).

There is a savage beauty about Anathoth, but its geography is also highly unusual in terms of our national history. You will doubtless remember that when King Solomon died the nation split into two kingdoms. We have

lived with that tragic division for almost 300 years, and I don't see the healing of the breach in the foreseeable future. I question whether Ezekiel's optimism will prove justified. Solomon was succeeded by his son, Rehoboam, who viciously refused the plea of his new subjects for a lighter workload. 'Jeroboam...and the whole assembly of Israel went to Rehoboam and said to him: "Your father put a heavy yoke on us, but now lighten the harsh labour and the heavy yoke he put on us, and we will serve you" ' (1 Kings 12:3–4). They took a psychological gamble with the new king, and lost. One new king is ready to be generous, another is too full of confidence and ambition to make concessions. The bread of the people was buttered on the wrong side on this occasion. Rehoboam took advice from his elders and from the strutting young men who had wormed their way into his company. It is one of the disasters of history, and we have known many more, that Rehoboam listened to the wrong group. The split could so easily have been avoided. The elders assured Rehoboam, 'If today you will be a servant to these people and serve them and give them a favourable answer, they will also be your servants' (1 Kings 12:7). The young men around the king were arrogantly and ambitiously short-sighted. Their message was simple: let the king tell the people, 'My father laid on you a heavy yoke; I will make it even heavier. My father scourged you with whips; I will scourge you with scorpions' (1 Kings 12:11). Rehoboam followed his young men, Israel rebelled against him, and the nation became two nations. Rehoboam continued as king over the southern kingdom, Judah, with his head-quarters in Jerusalem and Jeroboam became king of the northern kingdom, Israel or Ephraim (1 Kings 12:16–21).

I think you would call it an identity crisis. That's our problem in Anathoth. Anathoth lies in the southern of these two kingdoms, Judah. You'd expect that, when we are so near to Jerusalem, but in fact it belongs to the tribe of Benjamin, which sets it in the northern kingdom of

Israel. It's a curious paradox for the local people who at times seem unsure about where they belong and to whom they owe allegiance. For what it's worth, my opinion is that the traditions we cherish here are those of the North. I have made my own love for the northern kingdom very clear in the promise I recorded. 'I will build you up again and you will be rebuilt, O Virgin Israel. Again you will take up your tambourines and go out to dance with the joyful' (Jer 31:4). Yes, we also have people who would prefer to stay in exile if rescue means tambourines and dancing!

My father's name was Hilkiah and he was one of the priests in Anathoth (Jer 1:1). Dad's ministry as a priest is important in the story of my early life for two reasons: it sheds interesting light on my ancestry and it explains my family's bitter resentment towards my prophetic activity.

My family line can be traced back to Abiathar more than three centuries ago. When Solomon became king he removed Abiathar from the Jerusalem priesthood and sent him back to Anathoth (1 Kings 1:7; 2:26ff). Abiathar had supported Adonijah's claim against Solomon to succeed David as king, and he was made to pay dearly for choosing the wrong side. That dismissal by Solomon entailed the automatic exclusion for all time of Abiathar's line from serving at the central sanctuary in Jerusalem. It was a terrible humiliation, and we still felt it keenly in my early days. My father could minister as a priest at the rural shrine of Anathoth, but he could entertain no hopes of any red letter day in Jerusalem. There is a rumour that Abiathar was the sole survivor of the house of Eli and I might therefore be able to trace back my ancestry through the priesthood at Shiloh to the beginning of Israel's life as a nation in the time of Moses. I want to research the rumour because it sounds exciting to me. Ah, the pride of family trees!

Dad wanted me to follow in his footsteps, and that had been my expectation and my preparation until my call to be a prophet. You can't mix priest and prophet, and to choose one meant to turn away from the other. In one way I was more than happy to submit to the family plans for me, and I certainly did not want the mantle of national irritant which God was wrapping firmly round my shoulders. I had no wish to be a prophet, but I was aware of a growing and gnawing concern within me that the priests were impotent to serve the needs of our time. I smelled a corruption and a disintegration which were moral and spiritual. I was convinced that the priests were contributing to the decay rather than arresting it. Perhaps I was more ready than I want to admit when God called me to serve him as a prophet. My family were bound to take this very badly, and they did.

I can't tell you the exact year of my birth because we don't keep precise records as you do. We have no Hebrew words for 'Somerset House'. I'm told it was about the time that King Manasseh died, and I'm relieved that we never met. The rot began with him. With the benefit of hindsight I can say that the doom of our people was sealed in the days of Manasseh. 'I will make them abhorrent to all the kingdoms of the earth because of what Manasseh son of Hezekiah king of Judah did in Jerusalem' (Jer 15:4). Manasseh fawned in his subservience to Assyria; its policies, its filthy cults, its disgusting deities and its ruthless suppression of the prophets (2 Kings 21:1–18).

I realise now that I was destined to live in an age of turbulent change and to be an increasingly active participant in the upheavals. Kingdoms were shaking and the mighty were likely to fall. Public affairs, at home and abroad, were spelling 'threat' and none of us would be spared the terrible consequences of Manasseh's pitiless rule and the weak-kneed inadequacies of those who reigned after him.

I turned my back on the priests and I became a prophet, called in my mid to late teens to serve God. My family was hurt, upset and completely bewildered, and for most people that finds expression in angry outbursts. My parents were no exception, and my brothers and sisters clustered around them in dubious loyalty. This created enormous emotional pressure for me, but a young man must be free to make his own way. It is vital to remain true to yourself and I was stubborn enough to do that. I felt torn apart because I did not want the life to which I was being called, and I wasn't enjoying my family's reaction for one moment. It's ironic really. They had built tough character into me, and that was now the very instrument of my independence. The judgements they poured against me were judgements on themselves because I had so many family traits in me; obstinacy for one.

In time I was irritated by their refusal to appreciate the tension I felt about my prophetic role, and the total lack of support they gave me. I became flippant about them. I imagined my parents paying a visit to the resident psychiatrist in Jerusalem for counselling about their difficult son. I guessed what might be said on such occasions, and I pictured myself as a fly on the wall. Mum would pour it all out in high and immediate emotion; Dad would sit there smouldering in silence until he exploded. But I do have a sneaking sympathy for both of them. Their son was claiming pictures from the Lord, seeing figs (Jer 24:1–10); their son was doing weird things, wearing yokes and smashing pots (Jer 19, 27, 28); their son was betraying the priesthood and supporting those awful reforms of King Josiah (Jer 22:15ff; cf 2 Kings 22—23; 2 Chron 34—35); their son had suddenly turned against the family, refusing to attend any functions at all (Jer 16:1, 5, 8). The whole neighbourhood was up in arms against him, and they were bearing the brunt of this shameful unpopularity. Well, how would you have counselled them? Maybe they should have thought about the significance of Hannah's dedication of Samuel: 'So now I give him to the Lord. For his whole life he shall be given over to the Lord' (1 Sam 1:28). If you give your son away, you can't demand him back.

I was quiet for some years after my call. Sermon preparation takes a long time when you're a beginner! The Assyrian Empire was now into its terminal illness. Northern armies were breaking onto the scene; Nineveh, the capital city of Assyria, would come to its final collapse; Egypt's yo-yo history would suffer decisive defeat; Babylon would rise to unquestioned supremacy; Jerusalem and its Temple would be razed to the ground; and all this would happen in the forty years of my active work. For these forty years I would warn and threaten and plead, and we would lurch from one vain hope to another, living always in spiritual futility.

The flame of longing for national freedom burned to the bitter end. In these times mighty men crossed the stage and some of them have been truly great men of history: Tyrant Nebuchadnezzar, Pharaoh Neco, King Josiah, Prophet Ezekiel. These were the momentous years which ended the seventh century and opened the sixth. I have a sneaking if arrogant suspicion that of all the names I have mentioned to you, mine is the most familiar, and I am Jeremiah.

3

My Pictures

I'm nervous about your reaction to all this, but I've had some pictures from the Lord. No, don't take a step backwards. I can see the cynicism in your eyes. You've obviously suffered this kind of talk before. Well, so had I. I've cringed in sceptical embarrassment when others have paraded their pictures. But that was before my own pictures started to come.

If I'm honest, I've always been uncomfortable, and at times envious, when people have talked of the Lord giving them pictures, and I've discovered that cynicism is often the mask of envy. My own discomfort has whispered reminders to me of the scriptures which illustrate the various and compelling ways in which God reveals and confirms his word. It is deep in my spiritual history.

Joseph's pictures came to him in his dreams (Gen 37). Can you imagine announcing to your brothers and sisters that their sheaves of corn were bowing down around your sheaf which was standing upright, welcoming their homage (Gen 37:5–8)? My mind boggles at the prospect of attempting such 'sharing' with my brothers and sisters! Don't forget, Joseph wasn't exactly the favourite brother, even before the dream. It's hardly 'full marks for tact,

Joseph', is it? Joseph's response was to follow this up with a further picture from the Lord. It came in another dream. His brothers were stars, his parents were the sun and the moon, and they were all bowing down to him (Gen 37:9–11). His pictures were all the same. I'll be telling you a lot about my family, and I've had plenty of trouble with them, but I would never have risked these pictures on them. Yet God was speaking, and the pictures of Joseph were powerfully vindicated in his subsequent career. This does suggest that the question about pictures is not, 'Have they come from the Lord?' but, 'Am I meant to pass them on to others?' and, 'How can I be as sensitive as possible in handling such delicate revelations?' My counsel to Joseph would have been, 'These pictures are amazing, but whatever you do, keep them to yourself!'

Then there was Amos. I see him as a very down-to-earth man, not at all the type to have pictures from the Lord. He's exactly the kind of person to whom the Lord, in his humour, chooses to give pictures—and that's the man who should let others know what has happened, for the sake of his own humility. Amos produced a picture gallery of his own. He saw a plague of locusts devouring the grass of the land; he saw a fire, blazing and devastating the land in judgement; he saw the Lord as a builder, holding his plumbline to the wall, checking for an upright nation; and he saw a basket of ripe summer fruit (Amos 7:1–9; 8:1–2). The ripeness of the fruit indicated to Amos the ripeness of the people for judgement. In our language, the verbal similarity between the word for 'ripe summer fruit' and the word for 'the end' which the fruit depicted for the people, was so close as to create a pun vivid enough to make its own point to Amos.

I'm cautious now about cynicism with regard to spiritual pictures. I've seen how often the cynics are forced to confess to their pictures, and if they came to a man like Amos they can come to anyone. You can feel quite stupid when it's your turn, especially if your previous embarrassed reluctance is well known. I should know, it happened to me.

My first picture was of a branch of the almond tree (Jer 1:11–12). It came to me as I was struggling with my overwhelming sense of being called to be a prophet. My initial and continuing shrinking from this is well known, but I was totally unprepared for the way God dealt with me. He gave me pictures. In the middle of winter all nature sleeps. That is the time when the almond tree bursts into flower. It's a marvellous day when it comes, and it has caused the almond tree to be known in our language as the 'wakeful' tree. You see, the word we use for the almond tree is *shaked* and the word we use for 'awake' or 'watchful' is *shoked*. The similarity between the two words *shaked* and *shoked* was the point of the assurance being given to me. The sight of the *shaked* (almond tree) would remind me of the *shoked* (awake/watchful) activity of God. The almond is the first of all the trees to spring into obvious life at the earliest hint of spring, and we love it for its promise of better weather on the way. The almond branch I saw was no hallucination. I am sure it was a definite vision which the Lord brought to my spiritual awareness. Such pictures need their explanation, maybe you would say 'interpretation'. It seemed inevitable to me that this picture was indicating the watchfulness of God over the word of call which was summoning me and pressing me to a future so eventful and difficult that I needed a vivid image of his promise.

It was more to me than pretty and comforting. I 'saw' God's watchfulness and alertness over the whole of his word, not just its welcome aspects. I knew even then that I was not to be a popular preacher of revival, and mass crusades with dramatic results weren't on his agenda for me. In the almond tree, with its unique early flowers, I saw God watching over words of warning and judgement, words of political and spiritual reality, words of social and moral integrity which no one wanted to hear, but which cried out for a voice. Through the almond tree I would cling, often by the skin of my teeth as I'll tell you later, to the faith that God's word would not return to him empty, but would achieve its desire for his purpose. God's eye was upon all his words, not only those which gave promise and kindled hope. There were enough false prophets peddling one-sided messages of wishful thinking.

I could accept all this as the produce of a fanciful imagination. That has been my suspicious belief about others for a long time, and I have sought refuge in it. But that picture came at a time when I least wanted any revelation. All I wanted was to stay happy in Anathoth. And the next picture was so different from the first.

I saw a boiling pot, tilting away from the North (Jer 1:13–14). You know the sort of pot I mean, don't you? It sits in the hearth, large and bronze, and kept on the boil. In my picture it was tipping over—from the North. Perhaps I would never have noticed that it was turned away from the North if my mind was not already concerned with the trouble brewing in that region. I realised instantly that this was more than a picture in my mind. God was revealing himself in a way I could grasp; more clearly, more powerfully and more unmistakably than any detailed message. What superb economy!

As I watched the pot boiling, there came with it the explanation of trouble steaming in the mysterious North. It could have been the Scythians who were pointing up the picture for me. They did sweep down from the North, disturbing the Medes who themselves were on the brink of destroying the Assyrian capital, Nineveh, soon after the death of the last of the great Assyrian monarchs, Asshurbanipal. It's hard for me to remember precisely what was in my mind at the time, because subsequent events must have coloured my memory. I fully recognise however that this concept of an enemy from the North was a determinative factor in my prophecies from the beginning of my prophetic life. It is probably the first factor on which my prophecy depends. Certainly, the threatened collapse of the Assyrian Empire at the hands of these northern barbarians pressed on my mind the awful possibility that we too could suffer invasion from them. I've always felt things very deeply, and this foe from the North has been no exception. I recall that in one prophetic outcry I was constrained to plead, 'Let us flee to the fortified cities! Raise the signal to go to Zion! Flee for safety without delay! For I am bringing disaster from the north, even terrible destruction' (Jer 4:5–6). There are those who have described these words as unsurpassed in lyrical intensity in the Old Testament. The destruction I feared resembled a return to the desolate waste of chaos and emptiness in creation.

Honesty forces me to admit one more picture to you, but I'd rather keep it to myself. Those who mock pictures from the Lord have had a field day with this one. I saw two baskets of figs (Jer 24:1–10). There they were, unmistakable. You can't live in Anathoth and not know your figs, can you? They were at the front of the Temple, right at the place where some of you would put your offertory plates. One basket had in it perfectly good figs. They were moist, green and very inviting. The figs in the other basket were bad. Inside they were black and oozy. I felt slightly irritated when the Lord seemed to ask me what I could see, although it did appear incongruous in the Temple.

It would not have been a picture from the Lord unless it had an explanation, also from him. As far as I could grasp, the basket of good figs indicated the exiles who went from Judah to Babylon. Certainly, they were the significant people—officers and soldiers, skilled workers and craftsmen, and all those who were remotely regarded as aristocracy. God was presenting them to me as 'good figs' in order to promise his own power and care of them while they were in Babylon. They would be broken in spirit and

faith by this experience of exile, but he would continue to work through their suffering, and would one day re-establish them in their restored Jerusalem, but not nearly as quickly as the false prophets were claiming.

The basket of rotten figs—ugh! I can hardly bear to tell you about them, they looked such a sickly mess—were the people who remained in Jerusalem and Judah. They weren't good enough to be taken into exile. They had no future with men or with God, and would stay as the riff-raff of society. Zedekiah would be their king. 'King' I say? Not really, but Jehoiachin was in exile and his uncle Mattaniah was made king by Nebuchadnezzar of Babylon and given the new name, Zedekiah. I found him easy enough and he often consulted me, but he was weakness personified. Zedekiah was chief of the bad figs, and that just about sums him up.

My pictures were powerful to me. I'm not sure they were intended for publicity, still less to pressurise others. They did not create my obedience, but they confirmed and reassured me in an obedience already given. They always need testing and sensitive explanation, and are probably best treated as seeking my response rather than calling others to respond. They haven't changed my life, but they've definitely helped me in a life-changing decision already made. They have stimulated me to expect God's word in more varied ways than my intellectual pride would otherwise have admitted. After all, you could be in worse company than that of Joseph and Amos, not to mention me, Jeremiah.

4

My Visual Aids

They were much more than visual aids, but you might well be tempted to use that description of them. 'Prophetic symbolism' is the official title, and it may be quicker in the long run for you to familiarise yourself with this technical jargon. Although it baffles the novice, once understood official jargon does save a great deal of lengthy explanation. For example, see how long it takes you to explain 'eschatology' to a non-theologian without using the word itself! Anyhow, back to the subject, and no more digressing.

A prophet is a person whose trade is words. I was called to speak (Jer 1:7) and that provoked both my initial reluctance and my ultimate commitment. As time passed, I realised how often words could not convey what I wanted to communicate. It's funny how we speak through sighs, looks and glances, arm squeezes and many other ways. I expect they'll call it 'body language' one day. When I was desperate to give my message urgently and vividly I turned to actions. These actions were the message itself, and professionals now label them 'prophetic symbolism'. I was not the first and I haven't been the last to convey the Lord's word like this.

Do you remember Isaiah? I can imagine him, well over a century ago, running around naked and barefoot for three years (Is 20:3ff). He wanted to depict a captive. This would indicate that Egypt and Cush, on whom the Palestinian states were relying for help against Assyria, would not be able to help but would, in fact, be taken captive themselves by Assyria. Isaiah was desperate to prevent Hezekiah from joining the anti-Assyrian alliance with the neighbouring states; an alliance which he rightly saw as doomed. Sargon, ruler of Assyria, moved relentlessly and ruthlessly to crush the rebellion. Sargon's own inscriptions clarify the story for us. For Isaiah, his unclerical demonstration was no adornment to his preaching; it was an independent means of preaching in itself, and was capable of replacing the word. It often gave a vital and effective delivery to the message. I don't think I could have gone as far as Isaiah. I was isolated enough without running around without my clothes, but the action was a sermon, and I learned from Isaiah.

Ezekiel is, of course, much younger than I am, and he is still at the height of his unusual powers. I'd like to believe he was prompted by my use of prophetic symbolism. An older man, as I am, seeks no recognition, except to persuade himself that successors are walking in his footsteps, although they may travel further than him.

Prophetic symbolism was not merely a good idea for Ezekiel, it was a major vehicle of his message. On one occasion he enacted a siege, scratching on a brick of soft unbaked clay a sketch plan of a city (Ezek 4:1-3). He was in exile in Babylon at the time, only a few years ago, and he was obviously using the well-known Babylonian practice of representing something by a drawing. The spectators would have grasped immediately that this was far more than a childish game. I'm not sure whether Ezekiel had Jerusalem in mind when he depicted destruction, or whether he was anticipating the deepest wishes of the exiles by representing in symbolic action the face of

Babylon which was laying on the nations such a heavy yoke. Either way, Ezekiel would have aroused considerable curiosity.

One action followed another. I'd love to know how responsible I am for starting Ezekiel on this road, but he was certainly varied. He lay on his side for many months (Ezek 4:4ff). He shaved his head and divided his hair into three parts (Ezek 5:1–4). He visited Jerusalem 'in the spirit' and presented a symbolic picture of the false beliefs which held sway there: the idol of jealousy, the worship of the elders, the wailing for Tammuz and sun worship (Ezek 8). He dug through a wall at night, with the unmistakable declaration: 'I am a sign to you' (Ezek 12:11). He suffered the death of his wife, without mourning her (Ezek 24:15–18). That was an incredible act by Ezekiel, symbolic or not. He neglected all the usual tokens of mourning: death lament, loud weeping, passionate outbursts, ceremonial mourning clothes and the chief funeral feast to which the chief mourner was always invited. He even symbolised the reunion of the two kingdoms, Israel and Judah, in his vision of the restoration (Ezek 37:15ff). Ezekiel took two pieces of wood, holding them in his hand as if they were one. The great message of salvation was proclaimed through the symbol of reunion.

One of the reasons why this action, prophetic symbolism, is so effective for us is that in our Hebrew language and thought the word, *dabar* can mean 'deed' as well as 'word'. 'Word' and 'deed' form a unity through the one Hebrew word, and the prophetic action is thus able to be a powerful proclamation of God's word in itself. It is far more than a helpful addition to the word.

I know that some people have likened all this to a magical act, in view of our confidence that the action would be effective once it had been carried out. But that is complete nonsense. The power of our 'visual aids' lies not in their mechanical performance but in the Lord's command. His will gives them authority, making them an

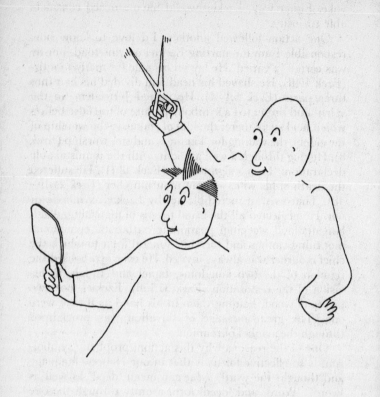

effective sign of his purpose for the future. That is the reason why I (and I reckon I must speak for Isaiah at least) spent little time worrying about the ridicule or rebuke which would be expected to follow such actions as I've recounted to you; and I am about to relate my own actions in detail. My motive was to disturb and arouse people who were obviously rebellious or apathetic. When you are totally sold out to God, yet confronted by people with guilty and hardened hearts, you snatch at actions which are strange and alien. Anything to bring people face to face with the God of revelation, not the god of their own making.

In short, my actions of prophetic symbolism were not sermon illustrations; they were the sermons! I wanted them to express the will of God in a mighty way, drawing the spectators into the action and forcing them to make a decision.

I forget the precise year in which this happened, but I rather think it was in the later years of King Jehoiakim. Not exactly my favourite king was Jehoiakim, and I was minded to prophesy for him 'the burial of a donkey' (Jer 22:19). He and I clashed head-on on a number of occasions, and I've no doubt that any antagonism which I felt towards him was amply reciprocated. Words were never enough to penetrate a man as spiritually dense as Jehoiakim, and he infected the people with his religious disease. So I resorted to action—prophetic symbolism.

I took a linen belt and put it round my waist, taking great care that it should not touch water (Jer 13:1–11). Then I travelled to Perah where I hid the belt in a split in the rocks. Some scholars have thought that I claimed to have travelled not to Perah but to the Euphrates. That would have been a round trip of 700 miles. No, I went to Perah, near to Anathoth on the North-East. In Hebrew we spell 'Euphrates' and 'Perah' in the same way, and that has caused the confusion and doubt.

Some days later I sensed that the Lord wanted me to

return to Perah to reclaim the belt. When I dug it up it had completely rotted. The sermon was that the Lord, through the message of the linen belt, was showing that the pride of the people of Judah and Jerusalem was spoiled, even ruined, although they had clung to him as closely as a belt around the waist. They had been bound by God as a belt is tied around the waist 'to be my people for my renown and praise and honour' (Jer 13:11), but in deliberate deafness to his voice they had followed their own ways. Those ways led unerringly to false gods, degrading worship and polluted living. My action was 'different' but its memory outlasted most of the sermons you or I have preached; and one thing is clear— Jehoiakim got the point!

You can become attached to this kind of preaching. Once you have found the idea, the preparation is quickly finished. All you need is courage and raw nerve. I felt that I lacked both, but I was so isolated that I had nothing to lose by vivid sermons. I longed for the people to see God and to return to him, and there was no way that I could turn back despite the heavy cost of my own obedience.

One day I was in the potter's house, watching him at work. I was fascinated by his skill, the dexterity of his hands, the shapes coming from nowhere as he fashioned the designs he wanted. Sometimes it didn't work, and he would bring a new pot into being out of the reworked clay (Jer 18:1–10). It was no children's talk which flashed into my mind, but a series of sermons, loaded with truth. If only Spring Harvest had been held in Jerusalem I would have made it on to the platform as one of the main speakers. This would be preaching—and with power.

Watching the potter at work opened my mind to all the ways in which I could apply his actions to the message I wanted to give. I heard the Lord speak to me. I was to go into the shop and buy a clay jar from the potter in order to smash it into pieces in public (Jer 19:1–2, 10ff). I can tell you it was an awful temptation to buy the cheapest jar of

all. Public demonstration or not, I wasn't that well off. I then went to the valley of Hinnom, where human sacrifice was regularly practised. Our religion had become so corrupted by alien practices that we were actually offering human sacrifice! The smashing of the jar would indicate that the Lord was about to smash the nation of Judah and the city of Jerusalem. There would be no repair. The accursed valley of Hinnom would be needed for a cemetery once this judgement of God took place. This sermon went down like a lead balloon, and I spent a terrible night in the stocks for it, but more of that later (Jer 20:1–3). This was an action of doom, not only highlighting the problem, but also pointing to what the Lord was about to do. Prophetic symbolism meant signs of doom as far as I was concerned.

You have to laugh at times, and I must admit I've often seen the funny side of this next action sermon of mine. It was serious enough at the time, and I had some pretty hot moments while it was happening, but it was the timing of it all which caught my sense of humour. Yes, thank you, I do have one.

Picture for yourself King Zedekiah, a vassal king of Nebuchadnezzar and a weak man at best. He'd arranged a state banquet for a large group of envoys from all sorts of neighbouring states: Edom, Moab, Ammon, Tyre and Sidon. He was anxious to make a good impression on them, no doubt hoping that he could make a bid for glory by launching and leading a rebellion against Nebuchadnezzar. I'd already insisted that such hopes of a brief exile in Babylon were pointless, and Zedekiah was in no doubt where I stood on the matter. I can't be sure, but he must have given strict instructions that on no account was I to be allowed to gatecrash his banquet. How stupid he'd feel if I marched in to denounce him in front of these snivelling statesmen with their sordid hopes for intrigue. It's my guess that he threatened the guards with the Valley of Hinnom itself if they let me in. Imagine Zedekiah's horror when I did storm in, with a huge wooden yoke hanging round my shoulders (Jer 27). I was so tense with my message that I missed his face, but it must have been a sight. It was worth my embarrassment to cause his!

I was dramatising my prophecy that it was the Lord's will for the nations to submit to the yoke of the King of Babylon, Nebuchadnezzar. At this time there was already a movement which aimed at the overthrow of Babylon and the liberation of the exiles. I knew that it would be years before that would happen, and then not with the consent of the king. I was neither a collaborator with Babylon nor a pacifist. I believed in the sovereignty of the Lord, and I read 'judgement through exile' out of the events of our time.

My arrival, stomping into the banquet, was my sermon. No words were needed, although I couldn't resist the explanation of my action. The yoke around my neck was intended to be enough. 'Bow your neck under the yoke of the king of Babylon; serve him and his people, and you will live' (Jer 27:12).

I kept the yoke, and when Hananiah, one of the many false prophets who were plaguing Judah, prophesied a brief exile lasting only a couple more years, I wore the yoke again (Jer 28). Symbolic defiance was my intention. Poor old Hananiah. Was he provoked! He stormed up to me, snatched off my wooden yoke, and smashed it across his knees. His face was black and contorted with anger. I must admit that for a time I was nonplussed and I beat a dignified retreat (Jer 28:11). That gave me time to think and I was soon back. 'Try smashing this one, Hananiah. It's iron this time.' There was symbolism in the iron as well as the yoke, and Hananiah knew it. He'd heard me call Nebuchadnezzar 'servant' of the Lord, and that was not said lightly, despite the precedent of Isaiah's description of Assyria as 'rod of my anger' (Is 10:5; Jer 25:9; 27:6). The iron yoke was a further sermon, not illustrating the preached point, but making its own point: 'I will put

an iron yoke on the necks of these nations to make them serve Nebuchadnezzar king of Babylon, and they will serve him' (Jer 28:14).

I believe in visual aids. I've seen their effectiveness. I've watched the point made without words, sinking in slowly, devastatingly, and I've rammed it home a few times with forceful application. No wonder Ezekiel has taken it up with such enthusiasm. I would use prophetic symbolism even more than I have done if I had my time all over again.

5

My Favourite Writer

I may as well come clean because it's been suspected for a long time. I love reading and Hosea is my favourite writer. You may have detected his influence on me in ways that I'm not aware of, but I will tell you about ways of thinking and means of expression which I have consciously absorbed. Imitation is the sincerest form of flattery, and this man has gripped me for years. To me, Hosea is not only a teacher but also a kindred spirit. We think and feel alike at so many points, and I know very well that I have immersed myself, mind and spirit, in his style.

Hosea precedes me by well over a century. He lives on in his band of disciples which has long survived him. He came a few years after Amos. Those two really were chalk and cheese. I see them as two people, totally different from each other, who are symbols of what God wants in the same group of people. Hosea—passionate, tragic, indignant, suffering every hardship of his people, knowing and reflecting the anguish of his God. Amos—seemingly cold, untouched, his heart far from his sleeve, pressing relentlessly the law of his God. Every group needs an Amos and a Hosea. Every group needs those who are openly sensitive and emotional, together with those who are calm, unflappable and able to stand aloof from the common pressures. I'm the Hosea of my group, and we need plenty of Amoses to balance me when I'm around. 'Amos, meet Hosea; Hosea this is Amos; make sure you appreciate each other, we'll never cope with either of you on your own.'

I'm tempted to play a party game with you. Each of you make a list of the influences of Hosea which you have spotted in me, and then we'll compare lists to see who has noted the most. On second thoughts, I'll tell you the influences of Hosea which I have deliberately taken on board, and you can add those which you see as furtive stowaways which I may not have found, but I'm sure I shall welcome them.

Hosea's marriage was a crucial part of God's word to him, and it strongly coloured not only his message to the people but also his own understanding of God (eg Hos 2). Hosea's wife, Gomer, deserted him for many lovers, and he took her back, a faithless adulteress. You can't read his passionate exposure of the sin of the people characterised as 'adultery', 'harlotry' and 'unfaithfulness', without saying to yourself, 'He's learned that through his own experience' (eg Hos 4:2, 10; 6:7). Hosea looked up from his own life and caught the heartache of God. We remember Gomer because she forced Hosea to know what God is like and what he feels. Hosea's marriage became a symbol of his word. That grabbed me, and when I became convinced that God was laying upon me a lifelong, inescapable demand to stay away from marriage, I only survived by feeding on Hosea (Jer 16:2).

I never wanted to be a monk. I would have given my right arm, not for marriage in itself, but for all that went with it: companionship, understanding and family living. I wanted to be a dad. But I saw that my lonely existence would be a vivid reminder that judgement was upon us and our future was being cut off. That judgement too related to national and spiritual adultery. Hosea's marriage became symbolic of the relationship between the Lord and Israel, a marriage commanded by the Lord. By contrast, I was commanded not to marry, but my enforced celibacy was also symbolic and I used Hosea's illustration of himself and Gomer to stimulate my own picture of Israel as an unfaithful wife who has turned away to lovers no better than prostitutes (Jer 3:1ff).

I responded deeply to the inner turmoil expressed by Hosea. It led him to know God. As he anguished over his wife, 'I will not show my love to her children, because they are the children of adultery (Hos 2:4), so he saw the heartache of God over his people; 'The more I called Israel, the further they went from me...How can I give you up, Ephraim?... My heart is changed within me; all my compassion is aroused' (Hos 11:2, 8). I doubt if there are any more poignant words than these in all of our holy writings. Hosea spoke to me and I felt something of what he felt. I made the cry of God my own cry, 'Oh, my anguish, my anguish! I writhe in pain. Oh, the agony of my heart! My heart pounds within me, I cannot keep silent' (Jer 4:19). 'Oh, that my head were a spring of water and my eyes a fountain of tears! I would weep day and night for the slain of my people' (Jer 9:1). Hosea moved me to see the horror of Israel's sin in her impure ritual, her callous society and her wanton dismissal of God's living word. It tore him apart and it tore me apart, for I learned through Hosea to see it for what it was to God, and we both shuddered.

Hosea had an eye for the false. He has become famous for his cry on behalf of the Lord, 'My people do not know' (cf Hos 4:1, 6; 5:4; 6:3). He complained that there was no knowledge of God in the land: 'There is no faithfulness, no love, no acknowledgment of God in the land' (Hos 4:1). He saw God's people being destroyed for this lack of knowledge. It was his most bitter complaint against them. Godly character and a righteous way of life were unknown because the knowledge of God in which they take root was missing. This knowledge of God was meant to include a practical application of the loving, trusting relationship seen at its best in the richest marriage. Hosea put me on to a similar scent, and I spoke as he had spoken. It was a deliberate use on my part of a vivid idea. 'The priests did not ask, "Where is the Lord?" Those who deal with the law did not know me; the leaders rebelled against me' (Jer 2:8). 'My people are fools; they do not know me. They are senseless children; they have no understanding' (Jer 4:22). When you 'know' God in our language, you are committed to him with a deep personal commitment which touches your whole life.

Hosea struggled with the tension between the claims of righteousness and those of mercy. He expressed this vividly: 'What can I do with you, Ephraim? What can I do with you, Judah?' (Hos 6:4). He reflected this struggle right back into the mind of God. Some have argued that this struggle is first found in me, but I was struck with it in Hosea. I made it my own in that I expressed it in a personal way: 'Is not Ephraim my dear son, the child in whom I delight? Though I often speak against him, I still remember him' (Jer 31:20). Can you imagine a higher, more poignantly powerful concept of God than this insight of prophetic doctrine? It came to me through my favourite writer.

Hosea went back to the days of Israel's youth when she first followed the Lord into the wilderness. He portrayed that period as a time when Israel's faith was uncontaminated by Canaanite Baalism: 'When I found Israel, it was like finding grapes in the desert; when I saw your fathers, it was like seeing the early fruit on the fig-tree. But when they came to Baal Peor, they consecrated themselves to that shameful idol and became as vile as the thing they loved' (Hos 9:10). 'When Israel was a child, I loved him, and out of Egypt I called my son. But the more I called Israel, the further they went from me' (Hos 11:1–2). I drank in that view of our beginning. I too was horrified by the enormity of our decline. We had sunk from initial bliss into pitiful squalor. The inherent sensuousness of our national life, infiltrating and corrupting our religious life, was utterly incompatible with the love, trust and thankfulness which alone could express well a right relationship with the Lord. 'My people have exchanged their glory for worthless idols. Be appalled at this, O heavens' (Jer 2:11–12). These are my words, but I'm sure Hosea would echo them.

You can overdo the search for the influence of one person upon another. We are bound to use similar words and ideas when we are dealing with identical themes. It was inevitable that a common set of subjects should arise among us as prophets when we were faced with similar problems of sin and rebellion. That's particularly true in the call to repentance which you can find among all of us. 'Rend your heart and not your garments' (Joel 2:13), summoned Joel. Five times in one chapter like a monotonous chorus, Amos reminds the people, ' "You have not returned to me," declares the Lord' (Amos 4:6, 8, 9, 10, 11). Isaiah's great plea was for repentance: 'Come now, let us reason together…Though your sins are like scarlet, they shall be as white as snow' (Is 1:18). But the amazing offer of cleansing was not taken up: 'In repentance and rest is your salvation, in quietness and trust is your strength, but you would have none of it' (Is 30:15).

Despite these inevitable similarities among us as we called for repentance, I was very struck by a couple of passages in Hosea. He depicted the people as making a confession of their sin: 'Come, let us return to the Lord…let us acknowledge the Lord; let us press on to acknowledge him…He has torn us to pieces but he will heal us' (Hos 6:1, 3, 1). Hosea was quite specific in one of these passages. He pictured Israel as saying that Assyria could not save them and asking the Lord to remove their sin: 'Return, O Israel, to the Lord your God. Your sins have been your downfall…Say to him: "Forgive all our sins...Assyria cannot save us.... We will never again say 'Our gods' to what our own hands have made" ' (Hos 14:1–3). I felt that such confessions explained to the people what was sought from them. If I could use something similar, the people would realise that I was drawing on Hosea and calling for a new act of repentance in our own time.

I used Hosea's idea three times: ' "Return, faithless people; I will cure you of backsliding." "Yes, we will come to you, for you are the Lord our God...surely in the Lord our God is the salvation of Israel" ' (Jer 3:22–23). If I could put words into their mouths I would do so, if only I could secure a new spirit. Telling people what they need to say can be extremely helpful, provided you can win from them a sincere response. I confess that I failed, but I tried hard: 'Although our sins testify against us, O Lord, do something for the sake of your name. For our backsliding is great; we have sinned against you' (Jer 14:7). I put it as clearly as I could: 'O Lord, we acknowledge our wickedness and the guilt of our fathers; we have indeed sinned against you. For the sake of your name do not despise us; do not dishonour your glorious throne' (Jer 14:20–21). These were the kinds of confession I sought from our people, and I freely admit that they are deliberately reminiscent of Hosea. After all, he is my favourite writer.

I think I've given you a sufficiently good idea of the way in which I've drunk from the well of Hosea. You will find influences I've missed. Perhaps a couple of brief points will be enough to complete my tribute to this man who has meant so much to me in a personal way and who has also inspired at many points the character and form of my message.

Hosea was obviously shocked by the adultery of the people. His shock expressed his sense of the horror of God: 'She has not acknowledged that I was the one who gave her the grain, the new wine and oil, who lavished on her the silver and gold which they used for Baal' (Hos 2:8). It was a puzzle to the Lord: 'What can I do with you, Ephraim? What can I do with you, Judah? Your love is like the morning mist, like the early dew that disappears' (Hos 6:4). I took hold of this and pressed it further. I knew of no pagan nation as fickle to their worthless gods as Israel was to the Lord: 'Cross over to the coasts of Kittim and look, send to Kedar and observe closely; see if there has ever been anything like this: Has a nation ever changed its gods?... But my people have exchanged their Glory for worthless idols. Be appalled at this, O heavens, and shudder with great horror' (Jer 2:10–12). Hosea's surprise became my surprise, and we both described the shock of the Lord in the people chosen for holiness.

The other point of link and comparison which I want to mention is the irresistible urge for all those who preach in the name of the Lord to borrow favourite sayings from those they most admire. I did this with Hosea. On one occasion he called to Israel, 'Break up your unploughed ground' (Hos 10:12). That captured my imagination. I spotted all sorts of applications as I pondered the unploughed lives of the people who felt they were faithful in every cultic requirement of the Lord. Unashamedly, I borrowed the words of Hosea. I wanted them to realise the origin of my words. I hoped they'd see that the prophetic plea was ringing again because of fresh urgency for turning back to God. 'Break up your unploughed ground and do not sow among thorns' (Jer 4:3). Unploughed ground is hard and unyielding. It isn't fertile and you can't sow into it. Unploughed ground is good for thistles and thorns and that's about all. Unploughed ground is neglected and wasted. But when unploughed ground submits to the plough, everything about it is transformed. I've no idea if Hosea saw all that, but I did, and I make no apology for using the words of another man. If God could use these words once, he could use them again.

There's so much more I could tell you, but I want you to read Hosea for yourself. If I have opened him to you I

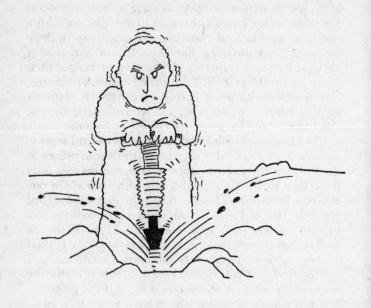

shall count myself honoured. Hosea influenced me consid-
erably, and you can trace this as I have traced it in the
areas of specialised vocabulary, the realm of ideas and the
unity of imaginations. I've learned wonderful things from
many of our canonical writers, but of them all Hosea is my
favourite.

6

My Struggles

'Cursed be the man who brought my father the news, who made him very glad saying, "A child is born to you—a son!" ' (Jer 20:15).

'O Lord, you deceived me' (Jer 20:7).

'Alas, my mother, that you gave me birth...I have neither lent nor borrowed, yet everyone curses me' (Jer 15:10).

'Why does the way of the wicked prosper? Why do all the faithless live at ease?' (Jer 12:1).

You may know the above as my 'confessions', but that wasn't the title I gave them. A number of passages are scattered through my story which others have gathered together under the heading 'Jeremiah's confessions'. The name is hardly apt. You will discover here a record of my inner spiritual struggle which is offered with startling honesty. But it was never my intention to make these experiences public. We can rush too quickly into an exposure of personal religious life. I was talked into exposing mine by my close friend and secretary, Baruch.

I needed Baruch's friendship and I have valued his counsel. Men find it very difficult to progress beyond the description of other men as 'colleagues', but those who are called to serve God need friends who are more than colleagues. I found such a man in Baruch. He knew of the record I had produced of my bitter frustration at the progress and outcome of my ministry—one rejection and failure after another. Baruch persuaded me to allow a wider circle into my experience. He felt that others would derive great encouragement to face their own failure and anger. He also seemed to believe that later students of personal religion would assess my contribution as of first-rate importance. That's not for me to say, but I do realise that if you want to understand me you'll need to enter deeply into my 'confessions'. But remember, it was Baruch's idea, not mine.

I do find the title 'confessions' misleading, but I lack a suitable alternative. In the official categories of our Jewish faith, these passages would come nearest to the 'individual laments' which you will find in such psalms as Psalms 22, 26, 35 and 102. I have broken the mould of lament through the sheer intensity and individuality of my own feelings and the anguish of my complaint against God. These confessions are indeed laments, but they rise from monologue to a genuine and personal conversation with God—and did he answer back? Ouch!

I can see why others set such store by these accounts of mine. 'Such conflict and agony of spirit have hardly any parallel in the record of man's spiritual life' is the way one man has put it. I am still deeply moved myself when I read through these personal diaries and remember the terrible darkness which closed in on me at times. Yet I would want to argue that the attempt I made to relate our national catastrophe (and its climax in the exile and destruction of Jerusalem) to the purpose and judgement of God will prove in the long run to be quite as important as the impact of my confessions. But who can judge the significance of his own life? It's a job for others, and I shall leave it to you.

My memory now is that of an old man, but I do not

recall that I related my confessions in chronological order. They were reactions at particular points of personal distress, and I found peace by pouring out my soul to God. You know you are in touch with him when you have lost the need to pretend or to hide. The confessions came from the earlier part of my work. They belonged more to the reign of Josiah than that of later kings. They express my spiritual struggles before I became such a public figure under Jehoiakim and Zedekiah. I didn't speak twice a Sunday as many of you do; I spoke when I had something to say, which was never twice in one day!

Later in my life I faced open hostility and persecution, and I'll tell you more about that in due course. By the time it came to me I was prepared for it, refined and stubborn in spirit. Strangely, active persecution doesn't produce inner turmoil in me; it makes me dig in my heels—no way was I letting their prisons and dungeons force me into submission. No, it was their intrigue, their gossip and their sly whispering which nearly finished me, especially when it came from those I had expected to trust. My confessions relate my torment in the face of this desolate loneliness: 'I am ridiculed all day long; everyone mocks me...the word of the Lord has brought me insult and reproach all day long' (Jer 20:7–8). I'm not unusual in coping so badly with slander campaigns, am I?

I have called the confessions 'my struggles' because that is what they were. If you dig deeply into them you will unearth for yourself the struggles which were churning in me at the time of writing. Better still, follow me now, and I'll spell them out for you.

I was struggling with prayer

I felt that I was forced to break new ground in prayer. Our cultic liturgy had become inadequate to contain what I wanted to pour into it. I wanted to plead for a nation whose doom I had been called to announce. My pleading would have been my own protest against the verdict of inevitable judgement which I knew God had passed. In prayer I remembered Abraham pleading for Sodom; but he was answered (Gen 18:16–33). I was told, 'Do not pray for the well-being of this people. Although they fast, I will not listen to their cry...instead, I will destroy them with the sword, famine and plague' (Jer 14:11–12). What sort of prayer testimony can you give with an answer like that? I'm sorry. That's bitter talk, and I should be clear of that by now. I was answered, but it was always when and how I least wanted it. Some see God's words to me in one of the confessions as the climax of them all: ' "If you repent, I will restore you that you may serve me; if you utter worthy, not worthless, words, you will be my spokesman...I will make you a wall to this people, a fortified wall of bronze; they will fight against you but will not overcome you, for I am with you to rescue and save you," declares the Lord' (Jer 15:19–20).

In prayer I longed for clearer vindication of my prophetic words. I wanted healing of heart and body: 'The heart is deceitful above all things and beyond cure...Heal me, O Lord, and I shall be healed; save me and I shall be saved' (Jer 17:9, 14). I asked for protection from my enemies, and I admit that I sought God's vengeance on them: 'Let my persecutors be put to shame, but keep me from shame; let them be terrified, but keep me from terror' (Jer 17:18). It was intended to be more than a petition. I was struggling through to a communion with God which opened up my entire inner life with its difficulties and temptations. I had to be totally honest. In that honesty I heard God and I found a renewed vocation which meant I was able to continue to serve him. But I was nearly lost.

I was struggling with myself

I knew that in these passages I was searching my own motives. Had I proved unworthy of my calling? People were insinuating that I was taking secret delight in the doom I anticipated as God's inevitable sentence. That caught me on the raw, and I struggled with it. I remember saying to the Lord one day, 'I have not run away from being your shepherd; you know I have not desired the day of despair. What passes my lips is open before you' (Jer 17:16). In my mind I heard repeatedly the concern I had tried to express, as accused men torment themselves with their own defence: 'Remember that I stood before you and spoke on their behalf to turn your wrath away from them' (Jer 18:20). Maybe I pleaded and argued so hard that the Lord wondered who I was trying to convince. I must admit that possibility has niggled at me for some time. Someone, probingly, has questioned whether I did at times cross the invisible line between 'an awed submission to Yahweh's purpose of judgement and a gloomy satisfaction in being its instrument and herald'. I feel that's below the belt, but I recognise a terrible time of struggling with myself and my motives. Sometimes we need to be vindicated by any means open to us. We're never at our best when we're pursuing vindication, are we?

I was struggling with rejection and failure

I doubt if there's a more crippling emotional problem known to man than rejection and failure. Or am I the only one who has wrestled with it? I could at times be quite content to suffer insult for the sake of the Lord: 'Think of how I suffer reproach for your sake. When your words came, I ate them; they were my joy and my heart's delight, for I bear your name, O Lord God Almighty' (Jer 15:15–16). Pious words, if you can hang on to them. But I was not always able to do so. Sometimes the desperate futility of my work, the total absence of any confirmation of my words, and the sheer refusal of the people to 'hear' me, drove me to despair as I was left a discredited prophet. And I blamed God: 'Why is my pain unending, and my wound grievous and incurable? Will you be to me like a deceptive brook, like a spring that fails?' (Jer 15:18). Those were the times when I was ready, even keen, to quit. I no longer wanted the responsibility and I longed to live a normal, natural life, full of the companionship from which I was excluded. The outward reproach of my calling had become an inner torment. But there was no exit for me, and no retreat. 'If I say, "I will not mention him or speak any more in his name," his word is in my heart like a burning fire, shut up in my bones. I am weary of holding it in; indeed, I cannot' (Jer 20:9).

I was struggling with ridicule

They say that the man from the East cannot bear ridicule. How many of you in the West welcome it? I had been prepared for ridicule and persecution in my original call. I'd been promised ample strength to cope with it: 'Do not be afraid of them, for I am with you and will rescue you'; 'Today I have made you a fortified city an iron pillar and a bronze wall to stand against the whole land' (Jer 1:8, 18). I thought I had my gloves well up and was ready, but I tell you, I was caught time and again with my defences down. It was the intensity of their malicious ridicule which unnerved me. They were contemptuous; they alienated me; they ostracised me; they plotted against me— blatantly in Anathoth and with more subtlety in Jerusalem. They made sure I knew what was happening so as to secure maximum discouragement and fear in me. You know where I ended up, don't you? Resentful and bent on revenge.

There is another aspect to these personal struggles which you should not miss. They are indeed my outpourings. I confess to recriminations, depressions, conflicts, agonies and outbursts. The one word which describes them all is 'darkness'. But I had to find God. I had to know more about him, not only as the God of my people but as my God. Ezekiel and I are such different men, but we have both fought our way through this battle, and it is with us that personal religion has become an established reality. Perhaps you only dare speak as I spoke when you walk closely with God, trusting his readiness for plain speaking. I do not know what future commentators will make of my outburst in the worst moment of all: 'O Lord, you deceived me, and I was deceived; you overpowered me and prevailed...Cursed be the day I was born!' (Jer 20:7, 14). I was pretty shaken when I realised that my word 'deceived' is the word used in our Law for a man seducing a virgin (Ex 22:16). No doubt the scholars will have a field day with this discovery, but they will only be horrified if they themselves have never been to the brink and tried to find God at that brink. Those who have been where I went will know, and they will understand. But I was going to tell you about this further aspect of my struggles.

In my struggles, God spoke to me. Sometimes there was silence; eerie, lonely and dark. Then God would speak. Let me tell you what he said.

'I ask the questions round here'

Why won't God be questioned? Perhaps it's because he is God. He always turned the tables on my questions, demolishing them with counter questions. It's risky to enter into a discussion with a God who calls for decisions and obedience, not debates. When I tried to say, 'I would speak with you about your justice: Why does the way of the wicked prosper? Why do all the faithless live at ease?' (Jer 12:1). He answered, 'If you have raced with men on foot and they have worn you out, how can you compete with horses?' (Jer 12:5). If you fall at the first fence, how can you expect to win the race?

'Your distress is too soon'

Today's panics are tomorrow's non-events. That's often how it is, and I was more than rueful when God answered the questions I've mentioned above with the reply: 'Your distress is too soon.' We could learn from his methods of pastoral counselling, couldn't we? He seems to be much more direct than the counsel is allowed to be which people seek from me. Do you find that? But our reactions are so immediate. We jump long before we've had time to ask the right questions about God's first call, about his present intentions and about his final plan. We are in such despair that we cannot see his hold upon us, and his way of glorifying his own name. I wasn't merely ruffled in my feathers, I was disintegrating; and this is the response from above. I would find all the comfort I needed by staying obedient and remembering his first promise.

'I light the fires and I put them out'

'If I say, "I will not mention him or speak any more in his name," his word is in my heart like a burning fire, shut up in my bones' (Jer 20:9). It was a terrifying word which God spoke: 'I light the fires and I put them out.' But it has proved to be a thrilling word, and very powerful in my own life. It has provided me with the question 'Did God start all this?' so many times. Once I'm sure that he did— by calling me—I go on, knowing that nothing and no one can snuff it out. The fire burns until God turns his hose on it. It's proved a marvellous test, and you may find it useful yourself. If no fire has been lit, don't waste your time trying to light one; the matches will all be wet. Our work becomes that of laying fires, believing that he must put the match to them. How I tried to give up; I wrote my resignation so many times, but I never handed it in. He had lit the fire, and he has not yet put it out.

'Hold together two facts—you are insufficient and I am sufficient'

My struggles were inherent in my call. I was not up to the job I was being given. You can be uncomfortably aware of your youth, even when you live in a youth-assertive age.

There's so much insecurity hiding behind the assertiveness. I started with extreme reluctance and my struggles reveal my anguished sense of the inevitable. In a strange way God kept me in that position of insufficiency. He did not allow me to be persuaded that I could achieve anything. But he called me ruthlessly, persistently, to his power. He would do all he had promised, but he was looking for faithful servants, not squealing kids. I was increasingly sceptical about my own role, yet somehow I went on. I was losing everything and could find no meaning in my personal plight, but I rested, trusted and went on. In me, man and prophetic task had separated, but I know that I was always a 'thought of God'. Nothing else matters now.

7
My Sufferings

Suffering often brings bleak loneliness in its wake, a fact that is not often highlighted when we think about tragedy and persecution. When we are bereaved we feel that no one has suffered the loss which we are experiencing. The feeling that *my* ordeal is more acute than those which others have to endure is one which I have known myself, and I've observed it in the attitude other people adopt to their suffering.

I have not been spared loneliness in my suffering. Those who insist, 'I know just how you feel,' are usually those who are least helpful as they unload their painful experiences on me at the precise time when I'm least able to listen. When I suffer, no one—yes no one—understands how I feel, and those who recognise that are those who come closest to me with a treasured ability to be with me where I am. They talk to me with their hands, their eyes, their arms, their squeezes, but rarely with their mouths. Yes, I know, this is the introspective depression which you expect from Jeremiah, but am I right or not?

I have told you about my struggles. They were the inner torments I faced for many years. My physical sufferings were different from my emotional crises. They produced a different fear, a different adrenalin, and they created in me a different resiliance to meet the hour. I was knocked around in the violent reactions which seemed destined to pursue Jeremiah into a premature grave.

Let no one doubt the power of words. My words brought me into all sorts of conflict and trouble. Do you remember my visual aids? In one of them I smashed a clay jar in public to demonstrate how God intended to smash a nation which had sunk deeply into religious adultery (Jer 19:1, 10ff). Pashhur was the chief officer in the Temple at the time, and having heard me and watched me he was angrily provoked. It's funny how adults catch the point from visual aids. We should use them more often. Pashhur sent his henchmen to fetch me and I was beaten and put in the stocks at the Temple, at the Upper Gate of Benjamin (Jer 20:1–2).

Can you imagine what a night in the stocks is like? It's much more than the cold which chills you to the bone after the heat of the day has lulled you into a false sense of security. It's more than the relentless discomfort which you can't alleviate by fidgeting, squirming or moving around, so that chapel pews seem like luxurious suites. It's not that you won't survive to escape with your life, because people don't die in the stocks. It is something more than ridicule, although ridicule is at the heart of it.

In the stocks I was alone. No one pleaded my cause or stood there with me. No one attempted to lessen the physical damage. During that time of mockery I felt wounded, scarred beyond repair. I was isolated and belittled, and the word of God seemed humiliated with me. Your initial reaction in the stocks is not to write a thesis or a hymn about the sovereignty of God! Now I understand how some of the psalms originated. All I needed was a short journey before I was thrust headlong into a smouldering resentment which thirsted for revenge. I began to question. I questioned myself, my call, my personal worth, my job satisfaction, and I questioned God,

angrily and directly. I wasn't getting things out of my system or off my chest; I wanted answers. I didn't mind what the answers were, if only he would say something. I know a small boy who called his father who was upstairs at the time. Father was slow to answer, but eventually he said, 'I'm here. What do you want?' Then there was no reply from the small boy. Exasperated, Father called back to his son, 'Why did you call me?' 'Oh, I didn't want anything,' said his son. 'I just wanted to know that you were there.' I felt like that when I suffered.

I hit back the next day, after Pashhur released me. I gave him a new name. It was all I could manage in retaliation. Jeremiah was never very good with his fists. 'The Lord's name for you is not Pashhur, but Magor-Missabib' (Jer 20:3). The name meant 'terror on all sides'. The power of such prophecy is akin to that of a curse, and I assured this Magor-Missabib of his appointed future. 'You, Pashhur, and all who live in your house will go into exile to Babylon. There you will die and be buried, you and all your friends to whom you have prophesied lies' (Jer 20:6). The boldness with which I made my prediction for Pashhur hid the churning fear within me. God told me in my call that he had planned a prophet's life for me from the beginning, and I wish he'd built into me a more efficient heat-resistance. But I steeled myself. If suffering was appointed for me, I'd meet it. Jeremiah will not be squeezed, and he's not for turning. On the other hand, I can't pretend that it did anything noble or refining for my character. Perhaps I missed the point.

There is an irresistible satisfaction in frustrating those who plot your downfall or your silence. I could be terrified, and I could be defiant. When I was stubborn I revelled in my refusal to be threatened and distracted from obedience to the word of God I was charged to deliver. I'm not sure that I fully understand my own moods and responses, because my original desire to avoid all controversy and to live quietly in Anathoth never left me.

Threats could reduce me to a quivering jelly, but a resistance grew in me which made me strong, 'a fortified city, an iron pillar and a bronze wall' (Jer 1:18).

Jehoiakim had not been king for long when I realised that it was preaching time once more. I knew deep within me that I had decided, with the arrival of this new king, to play a far more active role in public life, adopting a higher profile. I'll tell you more about that when I talk about Baruch, my secretary. It is not easy to describe how I distinguished the message God was giving me from my own thoughts and judgements. A particular pressure, a compulsion, a heart-racing, a sweating, and always a profound fear, all combined to give Jeremiah the signs he's learned to recognise. I could not prove this easily to others; they had to judge the words, not my physical manifestations. One of these experiences was with me now. God had given me a clear aim for my sermon: 'Perhaps they will listen and each will turn from his evil way' (Jer 26:3). Not surprisingly there was a sting in the tail, a characteristic sting: 'If you do not listen to the words of my servants the prophets...then I will make this house like Shiloh and this city an object of cursing among all the nations of the earth' (Jer 26:5–6).

Why do our religious leaders live on such a short fuse when they hear unpalatable things? It must be something to do with professional pride, as if doctors never need medicine. You should have seen them waiting to get at me. They were like a pack of bargain-crazy women pouring into a jumble sale. They all wanted Jeremiah. It was a strange, hypocritical reverence which persuaded them to wait for me to end my sermon. Don't interrupt the preacher, just kill him when he's finished! 'As soon as Jeremiah finished...the priests, the prophets and all the people seized him and said, "You must die"' (Jer 26:8). At least I knew where I stood.

Every instigator needs his gang. 'All the people crowded around Jeremiah in the house of the Lord' (Jer

26:9). I can speak calmly now, but I was terrified at the time. I was sweating, shaking and almost in tears. My mouth and my lips refused to keep still; they were totally out of control. I was in a state of shock. I'd witnessed mob violence before, and I know a crowd out for blood when I see one. This was not the time to stand on my pride. I needed some tactics. I pleaded for my life, reminding them with wafer-thin calm that I came to them only as a messenger from the Lord. The word, and therefore the responsibility, was his not mine. 'The Lord sent me' (Jer 26:12). I dissociated myself from the fate of my words: 'As for me, I am in your hands; do with me whatever you think is good and right' (Jer 26:14). I hoped they would think I was cool, calm and collected, so that there would be no benefit in frightening me. I always reckon it's worth injecting fear into an angry crowd which is unable to reason and can only react. 'If you put me to death, you will bring the guilt of innocent blood on yourselves' (Jer 26:15).

Suddenly, as if the fear of God truly had seized them, they changed. 'This man should not be sentenced to death! He has spoken to us in the name of the Lord our God' (Jer 26:16). I don't think I could pull this off a second time. They would judge in more reflective moments that I'd scored one against them, and I hope I would not be so stupid as to try the same trick a second time. Maybe they did have a change of heart; maybe they remembered their God; but it was a remarkable and very fortunate change of mood. You need experience to handle a crowd, and reasoned argument never works. I was obviously not as alone as I'd assumed. How often that is true, but we cling to our martyrdom with persistence. Elders stepped forward to remind the people that Hezekiah had not put Micah to death for his hard words of prophecy; why then should I be under such threat? (Jer 26:17–19).

I was allowed to live, but I had awful nightmares for

months. One of my fellow prophets, Uriah, did not fare so well, and he was snatched back from his refuge in Egypt (Jer 26:20–23). Jehoiakim had him killed, cut down by the sword, and I took the point. God had promised me resistance and hostility, 'they will fight against you' (Jer 1:19), and he was keeping his word. I had been warned, but I was in no position to heed the warning because God had called me to an obedience which transcended human threats and laid an obligation on my life which was absolute. In retrospect the night was closing in upon me and further abusive assaults could not be too far distant.

The initial exile was behind us, and we were now well into the reign of Zedekiah. I'm very reluctant to dignify Zedekiah's period as puppet king with the term 'reign', but I don't know how else to put it for a king. My relationships with the monarchy were off to their usual flying start—'Neither he nor his attendants nor the people of the land paid any attention to the words the Lord had spoken through Jeremiah the prophet' (Jer 37:2). Moreover, Zedekiah was now surrounded by hot-headed and reckless gamblers who were militantly anti-Babylonian in their outlook. They were keen to stake everything on a rebellion against Nebuchadnezzar, relying for that on Egyptian support. I was unwavering in my declared view that this rebellion was both wrong and doomed; and that was no way for me to make friends in the prevailing national climate. Most of the liberal-minded statesmen, who were among the 'elite' of the population, had been in the first group dragged into exile. I was thus deprived of the very people who had shielded me from the mob fury which had represented Jehoiakim's obvious hostility towards me.

Zedekiah was in a difficult position. Many of the people still regarded Jehoiachin as the rightful king. The Babylonians themselves described Jehoiachin not Zedekiah as King of Judah, and he was well looked after in his forced exile 700 miles across the desert at the court of Nebuchadnezzar. Many in Judah also believed Jehoiachin to be the legitimate king, and they longed for his early return from Babylon. Zedekiah's position was clearly ambiguous, and the ambiguity undercut the slight authority which he maintained. When the pressure for rebellion intensified, Zedekiah had neither the strength nor the will to refuse it; but I did.

The Babylonians at one point withdrew from their siege of Jerusalem. They had the Egyptians to sort out, and we could wait. I took advantage of this lull in the storm to plan a visit to Anathoth where I had essential family business to attend to. No sooner had I reached the Benjamin Gate than Irijah, the captain of the guard, seized me on the impetuous charge, 'You are deserting to the Babylonians' (Jer 37:13). I suppose you could twist my preaching to argue that I was a traitor in league with the Babylonians because of my views about acceptance of exile as the punishment of God, but you would be offering an evil distortion of what I was saying. I was stung and angry. 'That is not true!... I am not deserting to the Babylonians' (Jer 37:14). Irijah took no notice of my protests, and I was hauled before the local officials, beaten and thrown into the house of Jonathan which had a vaulted cell in a dungeon. There is no hurt like the hurt of false accusation. I was no traitor. I was the one loyal citizen left in Jerusalem. I cared deeply, uniquely, for my country, and now I suffered.

You will know the familiar saying, 'Attack is the best form of defence.' Eventually, Zedekiah sent for me and I was brought to him from my dungeon cell. When he asked me for a word from the Lord, I answered without waffling. I came straight to the point: 'Yes...you will be handed over to the king of Babylon' (Jer 37:17). It was a further chance to put the fear of God into a man. I challenged Zedekiah to tell me why I had been locked up in this way. Where were the prophets now who were so confident that Babylon presented no danger? I hoped to win him over to a more sympathetic view of my position so that I could plead for mercy: 'Let me bring my petition before you: Do not send me back to the house of Jonathan the secretary, or I shall die there' (Jer 37:20).

Sometimes your life is at stake and you panic. At other times you remain ice-cool and your words indicate meticulous preparation. I weighed every word to Zedekiah, desperately trying to control the rising tide of panic. Weak and pliable, Zedekiah on this occasion acted to my advantage. He freed me from the dungeon and prescribed for me the courtyard of the guard. The city was under siege and food was scarce, mostly available only at black-market prices. I was stunned when the king ordered daily rations for me from Bakers' Street (Jer 37:21). Yes, you're right, it was daily bread—what else from Bakers' Street? I was to be fed as long as there was food in the city. Things were fast running out, and it was an amazing gesture from the king. Weak rulers have their place if you can turn them to your advantage. Even Jeremiah knows how to seize the iron when it's hot.

Whenever things go badly wrong in a community or in an individual's life, a scapegoat will be taken. Do not be surprised in your leadership that criticism marches in from time to time. You will sometimes deserve what comes to you, but at other times you will be the much needed victim, the scapegoat, for the frustration, the envy or the sheer dissatisfaction of others around you. It will be the test of your wisdom whether or not you can discern the meaning of the stick you take. Accept the scapegoat role. It will be your offering of love to prevent condemnation falling on an equally undeserving colleague. I say this, not because I want to moralise but because I have reflected deeply on my own suffering. I became the butt in our national floundering for a scapegoat. I was the obvious choice because of the way I had raised my voice to interpret our plight as the righteous judgement of God. I didn't preach the sermons or live the life of one destined to be invited back a second time!

Pressure to stand against me grew for Zedekiah. Those who might have supported me were in Babylon, and the officials who remained in Jerusalem were sore about my activities. They knew Zedekiah would cave in eventually, and they were right. ' "He is in your hands," King Zedekiah answered. "The king can do nothing to oppose you" ' (Jer 38:5). These words aptly summarise Zedekiah's pathetic abdication to the court manipulation which took over his authority, and I was the victim.

I was seized again and thrown into the cistern of Malki-jah, the king's son (Jer 38:6). It was familiar territory for me because this well which I have made famous is in the courtyard of the guard. They lowered me by ropes into the cistern. I can still smell it; it was foul, stinking and rotting. The mud crept slowly, thickly, up my legs and surrounded me, firming in and possessing me. This disused well swallowed me to my waist and would have risen higher over me, but the ropes would lower me no deeper. Don't think I escaped with muddy shoes. In Eastern cities we don't call it mud unless it's waist deep! My sufferings were never noble, always humiliating. How can you make a hero's tale from being half-buried in a pit of mud? Mine was deliberate disgrace mockingly inflicted, and I was to look stupid as well as being tortured.

But if God has not finished with you, you are not finished. If he has lit the fire for you, only he will put it out, and he moves men, incredibly, strangely, to continue his meticulously detailed purpose. A man called Ebed-Melech—'servant of the king'—a foreign official in the royal palace, heard of my plight. He knew that I would be more favourably considered in Babylon than in Jerusalem, and he was prepared to challenge Zedekiah on my behalf. 'My lord the king, these men have acted wickedly in all they have done to Jeremiah the prophet. They have thrown him into a cistern, where he will starve to death when there is no longer any bread in the city' (Jer 38:9). Zedekiah swung again. He gave Ebed-Melech thirty men to rescue me from the mud which threatened to be my lasting grave. Your enemies never cease to be people, each with the potential for independence and mercy. Ebed-Melech knew of a wardrobe in the palace where there was the inevitable rag bag. Every home has one, however classy. Without these rags stuffed under my arms, I would have had both limbs torn from me. It was painful enough even with these supports, but I was hauled up, like an old ship from the sea bed. 'They pulled him up with the ropes and lifted him out of the cistern' (Jer 38:13).

I should have known. Zedekiah was scared for himself. Jeremiah's fate was incidental when the king was worried. He called me for an interview, but he was the one being questioned. Zedekiah was desperate for secrecy and for safety. He was scared that I would blow his cover and he was scared of the Jews who had transferred their loyalty and support to the Babylonians: 'I am afraid of the Jews who have gone over to the Babylonians, for the Babylonians may hand me over to them and they will ill-treat me' (Jer 38:19). I couldn't believe his blindness. Imagine telling someone whose persecution you have authorised that you want sympathy for your own fear! But men who are cringing and cowardly find this reasonable and logical.

Zedekiah turned to me. I gave him the advice which had been my consistent message throughout his dubious years as king. I called him to obedience to the Lord, to acceptance of God's purpose—active in the exile—and to a serious view of the warnings I was given for him. The very women who provided him with illicit pleasure at the palace would turn against him and use ironic taunts to mock him: 'Your feet are sunk in the mud' (Jer 38:22). What a lovely way to ensure Zedekiah remembered me! The outcome was that I stayed in the courtyard of the guard until the final and terrible day when Jerusalem caved in to the siege and suffered the total destruction of its life, its buildings and its Temple. 'The Babylonians set fire to the royal palace and the houses of the people and broke down the walls of Jerusalem' (Jer 39:8). 'Nebuzaradan commander of the imperial guard...came to Jerusalem. He set fire to the temple of the Lord, the royal palace and all the houses of Jerusalem. Every important building he burned down' (2 Kings 25:8–9).

The destruction of our city brought me freedom. Although I found that bewildering, I took my release and appreciated the options offered to me. 'Come with me to Babylon, if you like, and I will look after you; but if you do not want to, then don't come. Look, the whole country lies before you; go wherever you please' (Jer 40:4). When you love your country and your people, you feel a poignant sadness that your discovery of mercy and your offer of freedom comes from foreign oppressors who, as pagans, have laid waste to those from whom you most wanted friendship and partnership in total obedience to the Lord.

I have reflected with you on my sufferings and I have described some of them. They drove me in on myself, and yet I was objective enough to notice that all men were motivated by their own fears. Those with most power were those most afraid. They directed their malice my way, but it was not so much Jeremiah they sought as anyone who stood in their path; anyone who questioned them by whispering the words all men dread, 'failure', 'rejection'. I rose above my sufferings only when I had a fear greater than the fear of torture; the fear of the Lord. If I lost that fear, which was not morbid terror but profound reverence and desire to obey him, I was crushed. When I feared the Lord, I walked in personal trust, in defiant faithfulness, in stubborn loneliness; and I gave the words I was charged to speak.

8

My Secretary

Mid-way through my prophetic career I gained a prized asset, a secretary. His name was Baruch and I came to value his dogged friendship as a positive strength and a formidable protection from loneliness. The records of my inner torment remain mine and mine alone, but Baruch described the outward events of my sufferings with an attention to detail which I had no interest or ability to match.

I had not met Baruch before the reign of Jehoiakim, at which time I was well on the way to becoming the most unpopular man in the kingdom. There was a major turning-point following the battle with Pharaoh Neco at Megiddo where Josiah suffered a fatal defeat. It will be a mystery for all time why Josiah opposed Neco's expedition against the Assyrians (2 Kings 23:8; 2 Chron 35:20–24). I can only presume that the fall of Assyrian Nineveh three years earlier had raised in Josiah's mind vain hopes of a return to former glories. It was an act of insane suicide on his part, and he was carried away from the battlefield in a chariot and brought back to Jerusalem for burial. His son, Jehoahaz, lasted three sorry months before Neco deposed him and replaced him with his brother Eliakim, altering the name of Eliakim to Jehoiakim (2 Kings 23:31–35). In our day the view prevails that to change a person's name is to change his character. Would that it was that simple, I'd soon be dishing out the nicknames. Neco had imposed heavy tribute of silver and gold upon Jehoahaz, and he persisted in his demands upon Josiah's second son, Jehoiakim. I'm glad I wasn't a metal polisher in Egypt at the time. Jehoiakim paid the taxes, but levied them in full from the people.

Something snapped in me at that time, and I knew I could not turn back. It was vital to expose the current religious insincerity and to dismantle the falsely based political optimism. We were in a new time of peril and our rulers were pathetically inadequate to lead us through the gathering storms. I was now towards forty years of age, and as strong in mind and body as at any time in my life. My spiritual and political convictions did not change or falter, but I was ready to channel them into new and public areas with radical energy. I had come to the age when many men need to evaluate their lives. Much work lay behind me, but many years might lie ahead. I took new bearings and followed the results closely. I intended from now to be more public in my role, reckoning that the nation needed what it did not want—a prophetic ministry as influential politically as that of Isaiah of Jerusalem. I had to grasp the nettle, and I began with a temporary relish the task laid upon me. You could describe it in one of two ways: 'adviser in public and national affairs' or 'prophet to a dying nation'. The Lord was breaking down what he had built, and plucking up what he had planted, and I was the announcer.

At that time God gave me Baruch. He was a professional writer, attracted by the fresh stance I was adopting. We had not met before to my knowledge, but Baruch came alongside me and our close links of a professional and personal character were quickly forged. God has taught me to live in his timing and I have therefore tried to resist the temptation to lament the fact that Baruch and I didn't meet earlier. His eye for detail, for accuracy and for the interest of posterity could have anchored many of my initial sermons more firmly in their historical context, but I was never one for filing and dating sermon notes with records of when and where I had preached them. My sermon drawer was an unchronological mess until Baruch accepted responsibility for it.

Baruch became more than a secretary; he became a friend. I've heard other men speak with similar appreciation of their dependence upon such assistance. I found a secretary of such quality that a trusted confidence grew between us. He never let on to me that he foresaw my moods and reactions and planned accordingly. I did not realise that he had rumbled me, and he strategically hid it from me, allowing me the illusion that the initiative, the authority and the decisions were resting with me. It appeared to have happened unwittingly, but both of us were willing accomplices in the unspoken process which achieved a clear and outstanding working relationship. Baruch learned how to handle Jeremiah, and I was happy at last to be understood and even predicted. At least Baruch wouldn't want maternity leave when I most needed him.

Most men value loyal colleagues, but my observation and experience suggest that God is limited by a bunch of colleagues. The door does not open fully until the men progress from good working relationships to genuine friendships which no longer hinge on the work they share. We usually develop such friendships in our late teens and early twenties, often exchanging intimate and mutual confidence. Somehow, such relationships are allowed to evaporate with the passing of time, and I was not as quick as I should have been to grasp what the Lord was trying to create between Baruch and me. I now see that many wives need their husbands to find good friends who are likely to achieve in each other what wives can rarely manage for themselves. I would place friendship between men very high on the agenda for any spiritual community; much higher than tasks which appear to be more impressive, but I do admit that my judgement is coloured by the way in which Baruch entered and sustained my life.

Jehoiakim had been king for more than three years when I realised that I must bring a prophetic message of sufficient detail and importance that it needed to be put in writing. I was to record all that God had told me in the course of Josiah's kingship and right up to the present day. I hoped that the cumulative effect of the warnings I planned would produce repentance on the part of the people and forgiveness from God. 'Perhaps when the people of Judah hear about every disaster I plan to inflict on them, each of them will turn from his wicked way; then I will forgive their wickedness and their sin' (Jer 36:3).

I sent for Baruch and began dictating. It took us time to find the right speed, and Baruch was obviously irritated by my initial habit of dictating too slowly and shouting at him as if he were both deaf and stupid. It's a common fault I gather, and Baruch gave a good impression of patience most of the time. We worked steadily, and the scroll grew longer and longer.

When the work was finished I was hindered from appearing in public myself and I generously delegated the risk to Baruch! I asked him to go to the Temple on a day of fasting and deliver the message. The people would have travelled from far and wide, and a large audience could be guaranteed. A good secretary does not flinch from firing his boss's bullets and I sheltered behind Baruch's brave loyalty. The whole task had already taken more than a year, but I knew from the start that thorough preparation of God's word was essential.

Baruch read the scroll from a room in the upper court-yard at the entrance of the Temple's New Gate (Jer 36:10) The room belonged to Gemariah, son of Shaphan—a family which proved uniquely supportive to me over a

long period of time. The effect Baruch achieved was elec-
tric, but the bullets he fired were mine. A crowd of officials
was gathered in the secretary's room of the Palace, and
they heard from Gemariah's son, Micaiah, all that the
scroll had contained. It was like catapulting juicy steaks
into a lions' den, and they fell on it with relish. They were
like teachers in a staffroom, desperate for gossip. Baruch
was summoned to give them a private reading of the
scroll. 'They said to him, "Sit down, please, and read it to
us" ' (Jer 36:15). They recoiled in immediate horror as
they listened to Baruch. 'When they heard all these words,
they looked at each other in fear and said to Baruch, "We
must report all these words to the king" ' (Jer 36:16).
Then it dawned on them—'Tell us, how did you come to
write all this? Did Jeremiah dictate it?' (Jer 36:17). Baruch
was happy to draw me into the responsibility: ' "Yes,"
Baruch replied, "he dictated all these words to me, and I
wrote them in ink on the scroll" ' (Jer 36:18).

On their advice both of us went into hiding: 'You and
Jeremiah, go and hide. Don't let anyone know where you
are' (Jer 36:19). The matter was then brought to the
attention of Jehoiakim who was in his winter apartment,
warming himself by the fire. When Jehudi read the scroll
to the king it wasn't exactly 'listen with Mother'.
Jehoiakim was a man of few words and significant actions.
He listened intently to Jehudi, and not once did he interrupt him. Each time Jehudi finished three or four columns
of the scroll, Jehoiakim, visibly reddening, slowly and with
deliberate authority picked up the scribal knife, slashed
the scroll and hurled the offending passage into the fire
until every trace of it had been consumed. 'Whenever
Jehudi had read three or four columns of the scroll, the
king cut them off with a scribe's knife and threw them into
the firepot, until the entire scroll was burned in the fire'
(Jer 36:23). There was no flicker of emotion, only a defiant
fearlessness. 'The king and all his attendants who heard
all these words showed no fear, nor did they tear their

clothes' (Jer 36:24). His advisers begged him to heed our prophetic pleas, but they wasted their breath. Jehoiakim was bent on retaliation and he ordered our arrest, while we crouched lower in hiding. Doubtless Jehoiakim planned to stifle at birth a movement which might gather momentum and become a political challenge to him.

I was confident of one thing: our supply of scroll and our persistence. Jeremiah the author and Baruch his secretary would outlast the royal patience. We would keep going until he stopped burning; a visual aid in persistence. 'So Jeremiah took another scroll and gave it to the scribe Baruch son of Neriah, and as Jeremiah dictated, Baruch wrote on it all the words of the scroll that Jehoiakim king of Judah had burned in the fire. And many similar words were added to them' (Jer 36:32). I was rather scared, but I smiled to myself every time I thought of parents building up their children's bricks in order for the indulged little monsters to knock them over so that parents can build them up again so that children can knock them down again, and so on, *ad infinitum*. It was like that with the scroll, the knife and the fire; but Jeremiah is not supposed to be amused.

There is a defiance, even a recklessness, when two of you act together, which an individual rarely reproduces. Baruch triggered something in me without which this public phase of my life would not have proved possible. 'Behind every successful man there is a woman'—and a surprised mother-in-law. I'm sure there's also a secretary.

If you are as unmethodical as I am there are certain transactions you should not attempt without help. Legal business is a good example.

When I bought the family field from my cousin Hanamel in order to demonstrate my commitment to the future God would bring to our land I soon realised that I was up to my neck in legal minutiae, and I floundered out of my depth. I turned to Baruch for help (Jer 32:12ff). It was more than I should have asked of him, but this was the kind of strength I drew from my secretary. In our country the sale of property is recorded by a contract. This can be an oral contract, made in the presence of witnesses in a public place—as it was when Boaz bought the land which Naomi had owned, together with the right to marry her daughter-in-law (Ruth 4). The terms of such an oral contract are comparable in precision to those of a legal deed which will usually contain a description of the land acquired, the names of the contracting parties and the witnesses. I know that similar records exist on cuneiform tablets of such dealings in countries other than our own.

Hanamel and I had the contract drawn up, sealed and signed by witnesses, and the money weighed out. The deed was made out in duplicate; one document being sealed, and the other left open. I gave both copies to Baruch to be preserved in an earthen vase (Jer 32:13–14). I gather that duplicate documents were also drawn up long before my time in the legal customs and practices of Mesopotamia. I wanted to preserve these documents for as long as possible because I have some sense of the interest of posterity in such records and there is already widespread enthusiasm in my own time for family archives. The open copy was available at any time, but was obviously liable to be falsified. In the event of any dispute arising, the sealed copy would be opened and checked, and its contents would be binding on all interested parties.

I could have seen this through without Baruch, but that's my point. I came to rely on him and he never let me down. I trusted his judgement and his accuracy, and my sheer relief when he had taken things over produced one of my own worship songs. 'After I had given the deed of purchase to Baruch son of Neriah, I prayed to the Lord: "Ah, Sovereign Lord, you have made the heavens and the earth by your great power and outstretched arm. Nothing is too hard for you" ' (Jer 32:16–17). Yes, I know I've told you this before, but old men live by repeating themselves, and I dare not apologise because I shall do it again.

Baruch's faithfulness to me inevitably became construed as an unhelpful influence over me. I don't suppose that will surprise you. This too was not without its amusing aspects because on one occasion the tables seemed to be reversed. I was accused of firing Baruch's bullets!

It happened soon after the final and tragic destruction of Jerusalem. I had been given a certain amount of freedom by Nebuzaradan the Babylonian commander as to where I lived following the second deportation of our people into exile. 'Look, the whole country lies before you; go wherever you please' (Jer 40:4). I decided to follow his advice and I went to Gedaliah at Mizpah, staying with him among the people who were left in Judah. You never know when advice is a mask for a warning and I was not taking chances at this stage. Gedaliah had in fact been appointed governor of the land for the time being, and he was agreeing with my view of the current situation. Gedaliah used words of counsel which he could well have lifted from me: 'Do not be afraid to serve the Babylonians...settle down in the land and serve the king of Babylon, and it will go well with you' (Jer 40:9). The counsel was heeded at first and a plentiful harvest seemed to vindicate this policy. 'They harvested an abundance of wine and summer fruit' (Jer 40:12).

Sadly, the peace could not last. Desperate circumstances create desperate men, and Gedaliah was murdered by Ishmael, son of Nethaniah, in a plot which Gedaliah had refused to take seriously (Jer 40:13—41:3). It was more than a murder by Ishmael; it was an assassination in a bid for power. He had gathered supporters around him and the entire move was carefully planned. Ishmael was finally stopped in his tracks by Johanan, son of Kareah. Johanan had tried without success to warn Gedaliah of the plot against him, and he drew to himself the army officers who were eager to avenge

Gedaliah's murder and the killings which Ishmael had inflicted to buttress his bloody coup.

Johanan, together with the soldiers, women, children and court officials who supported him, decided to flee to Egypt in order to escape from the Babylonians. They feared that the Babylonians would vent on them their anger at the murder of Gedaliah, despite their obvious loyalty to the dead governor. The refugee group sought my prayers and my view of God's word for them. They pleaded with me, 'Pray that the Lord your God will tell us where we should go and what we should do' (Jer 42:3). I promised that I would pray about them, although I was disappointed that they were now calling him 'your God' and not 'our God'. That was a sign of the despair which had eaten into our national morale, a bitter cynical despair.

I did not receive an instant answer to my prayer, although it seemed to require an immediate reply. You too should not try to force God into your timetable. He won't submit to it. I waited ten days, and I felt foolish in the process. This was the time for God to vindicate himself, not to appear 'absent on leave' or 'missing presumed dead'. The reply was not unpredictable. They were not to flee to Egypt; that would be an act of utter disobedience. They were to remain in Judah, living for the future and keeping faith in their God. 'If you stay in this land, I will build you up and not tear you down...if you are determined to go to Egypt and you do go to settle there, then the sword you fear will overtake you there, and the famine you dread will follow you into Egypt, and there you will die' (Jer 42:10, 15–16).

They were furious with me. Having assured me about my reply, 'Whether it is favourable or unfavourable, we will obey the Lord our God' (Jer 42:6), the change was instant once my answer proved to be a disappointment. 'You are lying! The Lord our God has not sent you to say, "You must not go to Egypt to settle there" ' (Jer 43:2).

It's funny how they took back their Deity once they wanted to dissociate themselves from me. He was now their God and not mine! I didn't know whether to laugh or cry when they followed it up with this pearl, 'Baruch son of Neriah is inciting you against us to hand us over to the Babylonians, so that they may kill us or carry us into exile to Babylon' (Jer 43:3). Now the boot was on the other foot. Baruch had been taunted about the influence I might win over him; he'd been warned about working closely with me; now the roles were being reversed. Baruch was in the dock, and the bullets I fired were said to be his. Perhaps this was the final accolade for a marvellous secretary.

My counsel was ignored and Johanan led the sorry party to Egypt. I would have thought that Moses' exit from that land was a permanent word to our people that Egypt is no place for Jewish volunteers, but in our rebellion we learn nothing and forget everything.

On some occasions I had lost the last word, but this time it was to be mine. I kept one last visual aid up my sleeve ready for a time such as this. Baruch and I were forced to go with the Lord's rebels into Egypt. There, in Tahpanhes, I took some large stones and buried them in clay in the brick pavement which was at the entrance to Pharaoh's palace (Jer 43:8–13). I made sure that my fellow Jews were watching as I did so. Then I told them the meaning of my weird action. Nebuchadnezzar would come and set his throne over the stones I had buried, and this would be a sign of his appointed rule over Egypt and all who were in that country. It would be a dreadful time of slaughter and captivity, destruction and looting. Egypt would suffer as Jerusalem had suffered, and we had walked right into it, rejecting the warning of God. It was a dramatic and stark visual aid, requiring little explanation. Even here, my secretary was with me.

Many years earlier I had given my own personal message to Baruch. He knew how I felt in my torment for Judah and I knew I could express myself freely to him. In the fourth year of Jehoiakim's reign, Baruch had been hard at work copying out my dictation. I felt that God was speaking to him, and I rejoiced, not in the message but in the fact that Baruch was being singled out. It's so easy for a person with a secondary role to become accustomed to others receiving calls and words from the Lord. But his was a calling, a vital work, and he found his life's contentment in serving at the point where he had been placed, Jeremiah's secretary. In serving willingly he became the closest friend and the most trusted companion I ever knew, and wherever people know my name they will know also of Baruch. I was glad that I could say, 'Baruch, this one is for you alone. God has seen you and knows your work, now listen to his word.'

It was not an easy message for Baruch, but it did not lack all reassurance. God had heard Baruch's own cry and seen his sorrow: 'You said, "Woe to me! The Lord has added sorrow to my pain; I am worn out with groaning and find no rest" ' (Jer 45:3). I have discovered, as Moses did, that our complaints and cries do reach God. It's his response which is unpredictable! Baruch was to be reminded that God was overthrowing what he had built and plucking up what he had planted. Disaster was coming on the land, but Baruch would be wonderfully spared: 'Wherever you go I will let you escape with your life' (Jer 45:5). There was one condition for the stunned Baruch: 'Should you then seek great things for yourself? Seek them not' (Jer 45:5). There was an unmistakable sadness in the Lord's words as he vowed to set about a reorganisation of history, but not without a necessary destruction. When God is tearing down, let no man try to feather his own nest. Those who are close to God and to his people will be drawn deeply into this demolition, feeling its effect and its tragedy. Baruch was entering into the prophet's spirit at first hand, having learned his trade through me. I suspect that he, as my secretary, was able to trace out the sadness of my later years with such delicacy because God had given him this brief entry into its meaning. Baruch was led into the feelings of God, and that is a privileged part of the prophet's call. In the midst of destruction, Baruch's life would be spared. God knew that I needed him for many years yet. Baruch was the right man at the right time in the right place, and he was near enough to God to ask for nothing more. Would that we might learn his secret.

9

My Message—1

'You Are Living a Lie'

I was called to speak, and I had a lot to say. How do you summarise over forty years of preaching? Well, if they want to repeat their choruses, 'This is the temple of the Lord, the temple of the Lord, the temple of the Lord' (Jer 7:4), I'll repeat mine: 'O land, land, land, hear the word of the Lord' (Jer 22:29). That's 'my message' in a nutshell.

I envy Isaiah the enormous control he was able to exercise over his own emotions. He rarely pulled back the curtains, let alone opened the window. 'Turn away from me; let me weep bitterly. Do not try to console me over the destruction of my people' (Is 22:4). You need to grab that clue to Isaiah's emotional life, for you won't find many others. Not only were the windows closed, but the shutters were locked.

I'm afraid I couldn't live like that. The windows into my emotional life were wide open all the time, and you would have found it hard to disentangle my message from my inner life. Maybe I can take you on a guided tour, trying to bring the essential themes of my preaching under some general headings. I hope you'll judge that there's room for both Isaiah and me because I don't want to be left out, and we certainly need him.

I prophesied, on and off, for more than forty years. There were periods of silence, reflection, brooding and intense prayer. We prophets spoke often, but we prayed more. 'Oh, that my head were a spring of water and my eyes a fountain of tears! I would weep day and night for the slain of my people' (Jer 9:1). There was prayer in that cry, and I'm not surprised that I was forbidden to pray. 'Then the Lord said to me, "Do not pray for the well-being of this people. Although they fast, I will not listen to their cry" ' (Jer 14:11–12). He had decided that they were beyond such intercession and I was no longer to give my time to it. But hours of prayer lay hidden in secret. Those who pray are those who hear the word of the Lord.

'You are living a lie'

Over the years I have developed an eagle eye for false-hood; necessity has produced the ability. The capacity of people to live with every form of delusion staggers me, and a significant part of my message can be expressed like this: 'You are living a lie.' 'Truth has perished; it has vanished from their lips' (Jer 7:28).

False security

It can be shown quite easily that religious buildings make excellent servants but terrible masters. I spotted this with our Temple in Jerusalem. It's been our national pride and joy since it was built in the days of Solomon, but at times it's a mixed blessing, like some of those choruses which many enjoy in their worship; 'This is the temple of the Lord, the temple of the Lord, the temple of the Lord' (Jer 7:4). The people loved to sing it, chant it and recite it all together. It derived, presumably, from the early days when King David stormed Jerusalem and the defending natives, Jebusites, assumed complacently that Jerusalem was impregnable. They taunted David and his men: 'You will not get in here; even the blind and the lame can ward you off' (2 Sam 5:6). In their own minds they were sure: 'David cannot get in here' (2 Sam 5:6). Of course, David did break through into the city, but only by a brilliant and crafty plan. Jerusalem was a good place to defend, and its reputation lived on. It became linked to the Temple, supported by certain assurances from the Lord which were conditional but became treated as unconditional; a fatal error. The belief grew, fostered by wishful thinking, that Jerusalem was inviolable.

Isaiah added impetus to this article of faith. His preaching was shot through with the theme that Zion would be threatened but finally delivered. He saw this as coming not from military victory but from dramatic and mysterious divine intervention. The name 'Zion' originally referred to the south-east hill of Jerusalem which was the part where the old Jebusite city had been located. In time, 'Zion' came to be applied to the royal quarter of the city, and it drew to itself a religious meaning because the Temple was situated there. 'Zion' or 'Daughter of Zion' would therefore be a pictorial reference to the city of Jerusalem.

Isaiah loved to depict this theme in a dramatic way: a thunderous throng of nations attacks Zion; the Lord rebukes them; therefore they rush away to escape—'In the evening, sudden terror! Before the morning, they are gone!' (Is 17:14). Isaiah's handling of this theme paved the way for a marvellous call to trust and calm before the action of God. But in our day, as in times past, a great theme has been corrupted into a false security. I do not believe we can play fast and loose with great promises without a fatal flaw appearing in our corporate faith. There was no absolute security for our Temple, and the impression that there was bred a nation of ostriches, all with their heads deeply buried in political and spiritual sand.

Security in the Temple was a possibility, but not an unconditional one. God's word was: 'Reform your ways and your actions, and I will let you live in this place' (Jer 7:3). That reform would mean a new expression of justice, mercy and worship, a new integrity for ritual, and a new honesty for life: 'If you do not oppress the alien, the fatherless or the widow...if you do not follow other gods...I will let you live in this place...Will you steal and murder, commit adultery and perjury, burn incense to Baal...and then come and stand before me?' (Jer 7:6–10). God plans no time off for those who claim to be his people. The security drawn from the Temple increasingly alarmed me as false at its very heart. I saw it as a shallow refusal to face facts. A people who turned away from their essential commandments would find no security in the Temple. 'Therefore, what I did to Shiloh I will now do to the house that bears my Name, the temple you trust in...,' said the Lord. 'I will thrust you from my presence' (Jer 7:14–15).

I knew that God would never allow this security that the people found in the Temple to vindicate itself. Anything which can attract to itself such confidence will lure people too close for comfort to idolatry. I have often found myself stripped of all outward security so that I have to rest in a God who hides himself from me, appearing only through the word which he has spoken to me and which he called me to trust. I also concluded that the Temple was not essential to the communion of Israel with her God. That was dynamite! There was no Temple in the wilderness period of our history, but God was near to his people: 'For when I brought your forefathers out of Egypt and spoke to them...I gave them this command: Obey me, and I will be your God and you will be my people' (Jer 7:22–23). I have no inherent hostility towards the Temple, and in some of my visions for the future a restored Temple finds its place: ' "The sounds of joy and gladness, the voices of bride and bridegroom, and the voices of those who bring thank-offerings to the house of the Lord...For I will restore the fortunes of the land as they were before," says the Lord' (Jer 33:11). My emphasis was not on the

Temple or its cult, but on the Lord and his covenant with
Israel.

I devoted myself to warning and pleading about a false
security which would one day do more than leak, it would
split wide open. The Temple survived the first exile, but
eleven years later, following Zedekiah's foolish rebellion, it
met its appointed fate. Nebuzaradan, a commander of
Nebuchadnezzar's army, 'came to Jerusalem. He set fire
to the temple of the Lord...Every important building he
burned down' (2 Kings 25:8–9). I had taken my life into
my hands in delivering such a warning. I know of no
previous occasion when the destruction of the Temple and
indeed, the entire city, has been publicly and explicitly
announced. I was defying the priests and the mob. Amos
had managed this when he defied Amaziah, the high
priest at Bethel (Amos 7:10ff). I found no such immunity,
but I spoke what I was given, and I was fearfully vindicated.

False security breeds false assumptions and commits
those thus deceived to live a lie. It was not only the
Temple which sparked false security, it was also the exile.
Everyone was convinced it wouldn't last—that is, everyone except me. I was sure it would take a long time.
Ultimately, political catastrophe was just a small part of
the story, and it could be quickly reversed.

But unseen powers were at work, and judgement was
taking place. Men, religious men in particular, have
always scoffed at the suggestion that we can interpret
calamities and tragedies in terms of a God who judges. I
cannot afford to take such a soft view of God. My view was
not pessimistic or cruel, but realistic. The only valid
optimism I have recognised is that which is grounded in
God's word. In the exile he was unfolding a vital purpose
of national cleansing and purging, and it could not be
rushed. I pleaded for this to be acknowledged. All I could
see were countless quack doctors and nurses treating serious fractures as if they were minor cuts and bruises:

'They dress the wound of my people as though it were not serious. "Peace, peace," they say, when there is no peace' (Jer 6:14).

Hananiah illustrates this very well. He brought an alleged word from the Lord: 'I will break the yoke of the king of Babylon. Within two years I will bring back to this place all the articles of the Lord's house that Nebuchadnezzar king of Babylon removed from here and took to Babylon' (Jer 28:2–3). The people loved it; they clutched at it and vested real security in a vain word. This was disastrous politics and empty religion, which combined to breed false security. I could not hope to be popular, but I had to shatter these illusions: 'You have persuaded this nation to trust in lies' (Jer 28:15). I told Hananiah the correct score: 'When seventy years are completed for Babylon, I will come to you and fulfil my gracious promise to bring you back to this place' (Jer 29:10). 'This whole country will become a desolate wasteland, and these nations will serve the king of Babylon seventy years' (Jer 25:11). I warned him personally that he would not even see out his 'two years', and he died within a few months.

True prophecy is a serious business. It needs a health warning: 'Misuse can be fatal.' After all, this is a nation with a serious heart disease, heading for its final coronary: 'The heart is deceitful above all things and beyond cure' (Jer 17:9).

False prophets

No one wants to work in a discredited profession, and I'm no exception. Yet our land is littered with false prophets. I declared war on them from the beginning. Prophecy must be sifted, and those who have thrown me into the heat of the kitchen have been dragged into it with me. I have developed my own standards for the prophets, and they have brought me into head-on collision with my own colleagues. Such clashes were among my hardest battles, and they forced me to search for practical standards to identify the false prophet. Sometimes you can best achieve that by setting positive ideals and noting those who fall short of them.

A true prophet:

(1) HAS STOOD IN THE COUNCIL OF THE LORD

This conviction enabled me to challenge those I identified as false: 'Which of them has stood in the council of the Lord?' (Jer 23:18). How can anyone speak God's word if he has not spent time with God? It takes years to develop a relationship with God and to tune in to his wavelength. Words may not gush out in overwhelming spontaneity this way, but they will be worth hearing, and they will be accurate.

(2) HAS HEARD THE WORD OF THE LORD

'Who has listened and heard his word?' (Jer 23:18). This issue burned in me, and I often returned to it. 'Let the prophet who has a dream tell his dream, but let the one who has my word speak it faithfully' (Jer 23:28). I sensed the protest of the Lord himself when he watched what was going on in his name. 'I have not sent them or appointed them or spoken to them' (Jer 14:14). It's too easy to proceed on your own imagination, not least when you're committed in advance to pleasing the audience.

(3) HAS BEEN SENT BY THE LORD

You'll know that this is the essential consciousness of the prophet of God. In his life a call burns whose flame he did not light. It was the work of the Lord. Of the false prophet God says, 'I have not sent them....' 'I did not send these prophets, yet they have run with their message' (Jer 23:21). 'They tell them [false dreams] and lead my people astray with their reckless lies, yet I did not send or appoint them' (Jer 23:32).

(4) PRAYS AS WELL AS SPEAKS

I've already mentioned this in passing, but it's fundamental to the true prophet. I found this a devastating means of challenge to the ready talkers. 'If they are prophets and have the word of the Lord, let them plead with the Lord Almighty' (Jer 27:18).

Once you have established positive standards you can check out those who come with easy assurances, whispering into the mass ear exactly what it wants to hear. I saw the false prophets as the ruin of Israel. They were destructive shepherds, scattering the flock of the Lord. They were professional liars, promoting the adultery of national life. They were social and moral oppressors, godless in the very precincts of the Temple. I had three major charges against them. They were false in character: 'They commit adultery and live a lie. They strengthen the hands of evildoers' (Jer 23:14). They were false in their message: 'I have heard what the prophets say who prophesy lies in my name…How long will this continue in the hearts of these lying prophets, who prophesy the delusions of their own minds?' (Jer 23:25–26). They were false in their methods: I saw them as prophesying without originality or independence—'[They] steal from one another words supposedly from me…I am against the prophets who wag their own tongues and yet declare, "The Lord declares"' (Jer 23:30–31). 'They are prophesying to you false visions, divinations, idolatries and the delusions of their own minds' (Jer 14:14). They were passing off lying dreams as real prophetic visions. 'Indeed, I am against those who prophesy false dreams' (Jer 23:32).

I would do anything to avoid a return to the days which produced Samuel: 'In those days the word of the Lord was rare; there were not many visions' (1 Sam 3:1). We can do without a famine of the word of the Lord, but when prophecy begins to pour out, we must prepare ourselves to handle it firmly. Mine was no rejection of prophecy—I am a prophet; that is my only claim in life—but I will give

my life to preserve the genuine nature not only of the words of prophecy but also of the life of the prophet.

Will you forgive me a third falsehood which I fought to expose? To men of my calling these things work best in threes, and you must be used to it by now. False security, false prophets, and now....

False religion

Hosea saw clearly into God's view of our spiritual adultery in turning faithlessly to other gods. I caught his insight, and it is powerful within me. On one occasion I could contain myself no longer: 'You have the brazen look of a prostitute,' was my charge (Jer 3:3). The first point was: 'You refuse to blush with shame' (Jer 3:3). I'll leave you to guess the other headings, but how about trying it out for a sermon! It won me the 'Elijah Memorial Prize for Tact in Israel' for that year. Elijah inaugurated the prize and was the first recipient of the award. He won it for calling the king, Ahab, 'troubler of Israel' (1 Kings 18:17). Amos was a later winner. He called the women of his day 'cows of Bashan', oppressing the poor, crushing the needy and calling to their husbands for more drinks (Amos 4:1). Even Isaiah became excited and submitted his own entry, telling the women they were so complacent that they may as well streak in despair for the coming retribution (Is 32:9–11). It was a high standard of entry and I think my effort was as good as any of the previous attempts, don't you?

The work of the prophets has been a centuries-old struggle to denounce and destroy Baalism. It goes as far back as Elijah battling away on Mount Carmel, and it is a thread which binds the prophets into a continuous team, contending for their God and for the purity of their religion. I followed in these footsteps. 'Will you...burn incense to Baal and follow other gods you have not known?' (Jer 7:9). 'They have forsaken me and made this a place of foreign gods; they have burned sacrifices in it to gods that neither they nor their fathers nor the kings of

Judah ever knew' (Jer 19:4). A vivid and despicable example was the worship (if you can dignify it with such a title)
of the Queen of Heaven.

When I referred to the Queen of Heaven, I was describing a revolting cult which is clinging to our national ritual
like a leech, impervious to all attempts to shake it off. She
is the Babylonian 'Astarte'. The worship of Astarte, along
with other gods from Mesopotamia, became really popular in Judah during the iniquitous reign of Manasseh. 'He
rebuilt the high places his father Hezekiah had destroyed;
he also erected altars to Baal and made an Asherah pole,
as Ahab king of Israel had done...He took the carved
Asherah pole he had made and put it in the temple' (2
Kings 21:3, 7). This goddess—Asherah, Astarte, Ishtar
(she had many names)—was known in Mesopotamia as
the Queen of Heaven. She was an astral goddess, and her
worship was practised in the open—'all the houses where
they burned incense on the roofs to all the starry hosts'
(Jer 19:13). The children gathered wood and the fathers
kindled fires while the mothers prepared cakes to offer to
the Queen of Heaven. Late in my life, when many of us
fled to Egypt, they continued to worship in this adulterous
way. It was family worship of a vile kind, and I pleaded
with them to leave it alone. But to no lasting avail. Their
reply was to the point, and I did not misunderstand them:
'We will not listen to the message you have spoken to us in
the name of the Lord!... We will burn incense to the
Queen of Heaven' (Jer 44:16–17). I accepted the inevitable, but I spoke the word of the Lord: 'Go ahead then, do
what you promised!... But hear the word of the Lord' (Jer
44:25–26).

I recalled the days of the Exodus, and the amazing
provision of God's guidance and power: 'The
Lord...brought us up out of Egypt and led us through the
barren wilderness...I brought you into a fertile land to eat
its fruit and rich produce' (Jer 2:6–7). We had so few
religious externals then, but now we're surrounded by

them. Instead of serving us in our approach to God they have risen up as idols, becoming corrupted and depraved. The Temple, the sacrificial system, the burnt offerings, the ark of the covenant, circumcision, even our Sabbath—they have all become mere ritual observances; an empty parade in which I can no longer take part.

I'm no different from the other prophets. I am not rejecting all ritual, but I am condemning with all my powers a hollow sham. Perhaps you've played party games and panel games which have 'true or false?' as their topic. This too is my ultimate assessment of religion in its faith and its practice. We cannot major on a sales push or a 'rent-a-crowd' drive. Religion must not submit to the demands of emotions, instincts, pleasure, enjoyment and profitability, although crowd-pulling secrets may lie in all of these. Our first response is to God, his honour and word and holiness.

This brings us to the one question with which I've been concerned when considering security, prophecy and religion: *'Is it true?'* I have stayed in the council of God, listening, waiting, hearing. A detective's instinct for what is false gives me courage for a relentless pursuit at every point of response to God: 'Is it true?' I'm living for worship to be married to daily life as a transparent demonstration of the requirement of our God. Nothing less can be allowed to survive, whatever the cost to me.

10

My Message—2

'Don't Stop with the Superficial'

After Manasseh we needed a strong national laxative. I made a large stake on his grandson, King Josiah, emptying those forty-five years from our system, but I finished as a disillusioned man. I learned the hard way that you can't stop with the superficial, especially in reform, and that's what Josiah did. Maybe, with the distance of time, I'm ready to be more charitable and to recognise that Josiah took reform as far as he could, but the people were saying, 'Thus far and no further.' He never reached the grass roots of daily life in Judah, and I realised after some years that his reform was like building a sand castle in an attempt to prevent the incoming tide, the tide of religious and national degeneracy. We were irretrievably sunk into the kind of superstition which readily accommodates, and even welcomes, Assyrian gods with their more attractive and less demanding requirements. In such situations you need prophets not kings; and Josiah was a king, but I am a prophet.

Assyria came to the height of her powers while Manasseh was king. Manasseh saw the rule of Sennacherib, Esarhaddon and Ashurbanipal who was the last of the great Assyrian kings. He did a U-turn on Hezekiah's

reforms and returned to the pro-Assyrian policies of his
grandfather, Ahaz, an old sparring partner of Isaiah (2
Kings 21:1–17; Is 7:1–17). 'Pro-Assyria' doesn't mean
gentle support and friendship where we live. It means
grovelling and creeping and paying heavy tribute. The
religious consequences defy description because they were
the focal point of the political surrender being made. Local
shrines were restored, and pagan practices invaded these
shrines. Fertility cults and 'sacred' prostitution moved
into the Temple precincts. The final outrage was the
acceptance of the cult of Molech with its human sacrifices.
Former Canaanite practices had a field day of a come-
back, and their disgusting symbol, the Asherah pole, was
reintroduced. Into these conditions Josiah was born, and I
too arrived on the scene. When Josiah was eight years old,
his father Amon was assassinated after only two years as
king (2 Kings 21:19–24).

The death of Ashurbanipal came at a time when Josiah
was about twenty-one years old. That's the age when a
man is ready to try his powers and to be daring where
caution might restrain an older man. Josiah was ready to
bring our people to independence from Assyria whose far-
flung empire was on the verge of collapse.

You will have access to two accounts of Josiah's reforms
(2 Kings 22–23; 2 Chron 34–35). All I can do is give you
my version of events and trace my grasp of Josiah's work
as an attempt at thorough decoration which turned out to
do no more than paper over the cracks. I saw in time that
these cracks were gaping splits, and that's no way to hang
the paper.

Around the twelfth year of his reign Josiah initiated a
series of reforms. They took the form of cult purification,
purging Judah and Jerusalem of high places, Asherah
poles, carved idols and images. Josiah had the Baal altars
smashed down and scattered in pieces over the tombs of
those who had sacrificed to them. The actions were religious, but the motivation was political. This was a firm

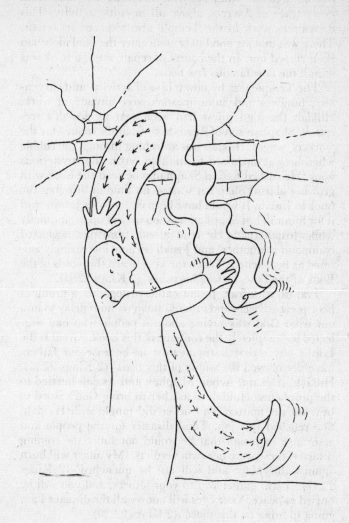

bid for freedom from Assyria, cleansing our land from every trace of Assyria, above all in cultic activity. This demolition work in the Temple also required its repair. There was making good to be done once the Baal idols had been ripped out. In the course of repair work, a book was found: the now famous law book.

The Temple was by now a hive of activity, and carpenters, builders and stone masons were already at work. Hilkiah the high priest had been sent by Josiah's secretary, Shaphan son of Azaliah, to fetch the money for the workers' wages. Hilkiah was searching through the rubble when he was surprised to stumble across this mysterious book. He rushed to find Shaphan who read the book with growing alarm. Shaphan wasted no time in bringing the book to Josiah. It would have been easier to let Josiah read it for himself, but Shaphan was too wound up to sit quietly while Josiah read. He read aloud, from one neglected command to another, and Josiah became increasingly agitated as he listened. 'When the king heard the words of the Book of the Law, he tore his robes' (2 Kings 22:11).

Frantic with fear, Josiah gathered together a group of his closest advisers and ordered them without delay to find out what God was saying about a people who had neglected so completely the contents of this book. 'Great is the Lord's anger that burns against us because our fathers have not obeyed the words of this book' (2 Kings 22:13). Hilkiah, Ahikam, Acbor, Shaphan and Asaiah hurried to the prophetess Huldah to ask her to bring God's word to bear on the matter. You never did tangle with Huldah. She relished this job. Total disaster for the people and assurance to Josiah that he would not suffer the coming disaster; these were her twin verdicts. 'My anger will burn against this place and will not be quenched' (2 Kings 22:17). 'I will gather you to your fathers, and you will be buried in peace. Your eyes will not see all the disaster I am going to bring on this place' (2 Kings 22:20).

This was a matter of urgency. Josiah called together

priests, prophets and people. They met at the Temple, and he read to them the requirements of the book which had been found, calling the people to be with him in a new covenant of obedience and loyalty to the law book and to its God. The discovery of the law book was not initiating reform, but giving an existing reform new impetus and new direction. It needs to be recognised that the contents of the law book were identical to some of the requirements of a book already in existence, known now as Deuteronomy. Deuteronomy was the product of a group from the northern kingdom with a passion for religious reform. They had grown increasingly despondent in the reign of Manasseh, and their hearts yearned for a new day of faithfulness to the religion of our fathers. They looked for such a man as Hezekiah had been to launch a fresh time of renewal. Realising in Josiah's eighteenth year, the year the law book was found, that reform would continue, they welcomed unreservedly the work he had begun and committed themselves to see him as their ally. The finding of the law book would bring new authority for what might have been done in a less systematic way solely on the precedent of Hezekiah's reforms. The stipulations of the law book which were put into effect are the stipulations also of Deuteronomy.

The removal of all objects connected with the Baal cult was intensified to the point of completion. They were burned publicly in the fields of the Kidron Valley. Every official of these practices was thrown out of work, including the cult prostitutes. All local shrines were abolished, even the altar at Bethel. The cult was thus centralised at Jerusalem. Then Josiah ordered the recovery of the Feast of Passover. 'The king gave this order to all the people, "Celebrate the Passover to the Lord your God, as it is written in this Book of the Covenant" ' (2 Kings 23:21). The Passover had been ignored since the days of the judges, and we saw it restored in Jerusalem. 'In the

eighteenth year of King Josiah, this Passover was cele-
brated to the Lord in Jerusalem' (2 Kings 23:23).

I, of course, was not in any way consulted by Josiah
about his reforms. At that time I was without any recognition or influence. Huldah had some official standing as a
prophetess, and I had no established record of vindicated
prophecy. But I welcomed with genuine enthusiasm what
was happening. My hope was that the purified ritual
would be accompanied by a changed heart and spirit. The
process of my disillusionment is still painful to recall. It
was gradual but sure once it set in.

Naturally, I was excited at first. I was delighted to see
the Assyrian pollution of our religion and society being
checked, and I could envisage a great gain in centralising
worship in Jerusalem. The easy-going tolerance of some of
our country priests had been a terrible compromise of
truth and purity. My support for these reforms did me no
good at home where the redundancy of local shrines and
their officials caused serious family hardship. They plotted
angrily against me: 'Let us cut him off from the land of the
living, that his name be remembered no more' (Jer 11:19).
So you think you have family rows! I still hoped the reform
would work, and I gave it my full support: 'Listen to the
terms of this covenant... "Cursed is the man who does not
obey the terms of this covenant"' (Jer 11:2–3). I was
referring to the covenant inaugurated by Josiah.

My own view is that Josiah ran out of steam, much as I
value his attempt at reform. I once challenged his son,
Shallum (or Jehoahaz), about his record compared with
his father's: 'For this is what the Lord says about Shallum
son of Josiah... "He will never return. He will die in the
place where they have led him captive... Woe to him who
builds his palace by unrighteousness... [Your father] did
what was right and just... He defended the cause of the
poor and needy... Is that not what it means to know me?"
declares the Lord' (Jer 22:11–16).

Following the reforms according to the law book, and

that part of Deuteronomy which it contained, Josiah did little more until his untimely death twelve years later at the battle of Megiddo by the hands of Pharaoh Neco (2 Kings 23:29; 2 Chron 35:20–24). Josiah was first and foremost a king, and he could live with compromise. His reforms showed how quickly the sincere can become the superficial, and the superficial the sham. They were directed more to effective kingship than to spiritual holiness. Josiah and I could see the Temple court crowded with milling, jostling worshippers, but he delighted in it as a demonstration of the overthrow of Assyrian authority and influence. I, on the contrary, was horrified that this worship was not linked to appropriate daily life, which for me violated both the Temple and its God. The reforming movement meant well, but I've always reckoned that 'he means well' is more a condemnation than a congratulation, as if there's nothing else to compliment.

Josiah's reform halted the worship of the Queen of Heaven, but it never tore allegiance to this degrading paganism from the heart of the people. Deuteronomy put it this way: 'Circumcise your hearts, therefore, and do not be stiff-necked any longer' (Deut 10:16). I followed suit: 'Circumcise yourselves to the Lord, circumcise your hearts, you men of Judah and people of Jerusalem' (Jer 4:4). This circumcision was for women as well as men. The plea fell on deaf ears, and it was made brutally clear to me that most people regarded the reform of Josiah as a discredited failure. I watched over a determined drift back to former ways. Manasseh had reversed Hezekiah's reforms, and Jehoiakim allowed such a reversal of Josiah's, although he did not promote it in the active way that Manasseh had pursued. The people put it bluntly to me: 'We will burn incense to the Queen of Heaven' (Jer 44:17).

During the siege of Jerusalem by Nebuchadnezzar of Babylon, the people in the city released their slaves and later dragged them back into slavery. I rebuked them in no uncertain terms: 'This is what the Lord, the God of Israel, says: "...you have turned around and profaned my name" ' (Jer 34:13, 16). I reminded them of the covenant made with God which promised the release of slaves every sixth year: 'After he has served you six years, you must let him go free' (Jer 34:14; cf Ex 21:2). As far as I was concerned that covenant included female slaves as well as male. The original covenant made with Moses at Sinai carefully excluded female slaves from this possibility of freedom—'only the man shall go free' (Ex 21:4). My reference was to the covenant of Deuteronomy which did include female slaves—'If a fellow Hebrew, a man or woman, is sold to you and he serves you six years, in the seventh year you must let him go free' (Deut 15:12). This covenant was renewed by Josiah and the people on their discovery and reading of the law book in the Temple. I found it both heartbreaking and offensive that this reform so recently adopted was quickly set aside once its require- ments began to prove inconvenient and expensive. There never was anything like the crunch on the pocket to sift a person's sincerity.

These sorts of events forced me to admit that the reform of Josiah was not only ineffective to fulfil my vision for our nation, it was in fact finished. Such vitality as Josiah had given to the reform during his reign drained from it at his death, which dealt the final blow to something for which I had held high hopes in the beginning. In retrospect, it was never going to be thorough or lasting.

'How can you say, "We are wise, for we have the law of the Lord," when actually the lying pen of the scribes has handled it falsely?' (Jer 8:8). Superficial measures will never change stubborn minds; they cannot cure perpetual backsliding, and they do not produce a return to those 'ancient paths' which set before us 'the good way' (Jer 6:16).

I never broke finally with the reforming party, as the loyalty that Shaphan's family gave me throughout my life

indicates: 'Furthermore, Ahikam son of Shaphan supported Jeremiah, and so he was not handed over to the
people to be put to death' (Jer 26:24). Yet inwardly I was
more and more isolated from them. I know that Ezekiel
views the situation as I do: a short-lived reform collapsed
with the death of its initiator, Josiah; its spiritual failure
provoking our condemnation of its insufficiency. External
conformity without inward change is not reform, it is
deceptive illusion, and any self-respecting prophet will
distinguish the shallow from the profound, as I did in the
wake of the reforms of Josiah. You can't stop with the
superficial, not if you take a serious view of the living God.

II

My Message—3

'Go with God'

Our sails were set against the wind of God. I knew this would slow us down; moreover, it was dangerous and could prove fatal. You can swim against the tide, but if you're in the sea of God you'd better go with it.

One of my major emphases was that we had to 'go with God'.

I judged the exile from Jerusalem to be politically inevitable. We were a nation in decay, and the disintegration of every form of public and personal life was in process for many years before Nebuchadnezzar struck the final blow in Jerusalem. When the first deportation of leaders, soldiers and craftsmen was forced upon us and Nebuchadnezzar replaced Johoiachin with his uncle Mattaniah, renaming him Zedekiah, there was a widespread optimism that the calamity would be brief. Men and women clung desperately to their hopes: 'Very soon now the articles from the Lord's house will be brought back from Babylon' (Jer 27:16). But I could give them no support or encouragement: 'This is what the Lord says: I am about to hand this city over to the Babylonians and to Nebuchadnezzar king of Babylon, who will capture it' (Jer 32:28). 'Do not let the prophets and diviners among you deceive you. Do not listen to the dreams you encourage them to have' (Jer 29:8). I could see no reason for these hopes which represented only a crazy refusal to accept the circumstances and to look for God's longer-term purpose. Acceptance of tragedy is the usual prelude to healing from its damage, and we were unable to come to acceptance.

I was not making a mere political judgement. Prophets are first and foremost men of God. We are politicians only because our message cannot be excluded from any area of human life, and in the whole of Israel, politics and religion are inextricably linked. I did see the exile as a political certainty. Once Josiah was killed at Megiddo the writing was on the wall; in fact we were a doomed people. First Egypt and then Babylon overran us, as a lion takes its prey. But I saw God as Lord of this movement in time. This was his action upon the people whom he had called to serve him, yet who for generations had proved guilty of unbelief, apostasy and spiritual adultery. 'You performed miraculous signs and wonders in Egypt and have continued them to this day' (Jer 32:20) was my view of history, but I could not secure the response I wanted from the nation: 'Let us lie down in our shame, and let our disgrace cover us. We have sinned against the Lord our God, both we and our fathers; from our youth till this day we have not obeyed the Lord our God...surely in the Lord our God is the salvation of Israel' (Jer 3:25, 23). Now God had chosen to use the exile for our judgement and our cleansing, and all resistance and resentment would be pointless. Hence my message, 'Go with God.' It's an essential message in far wider circumstances than those I am describing to you.

If you find out what God is saying and doing, and go with it, there can come to you an awareness of destiny and great calm, even in the kind of catastrophe we experienced. My message 'go with God' was vital for the hour, but it largely went unheeded. But let no one say I did not sound the trumpet. As Ezekiel fixed his mind on

Jerusalem, although in exile (eg Ezek 1:1; 4:1; 8:3; 16:1ff),
so I fixed mine for a time on the exiles. I'll tell you how I
brought this message, because it caused an enormous fuss
at the time.

I wrote a letter to the exiles

When you're angry, distressed and suffering tragedy, you
need a long-term view or the counsel of someone able to
take that view for you. I took a long-term view of the exile,
knowing full well that I was almost on my own. I wrote a
letter to the exiles which I knew would devastate them,
but it was their only hope (Jer 29). The essence of my
letter was very simple. It was addressed to all the religious
leaders of the people—elders, prophets and priests—who
were by now in Babylon. I sent it using Elasah and the
ever faithful Gemariah as postmen. I called for a total
acceptance of their new life in Babylon. Let them make a
new home in a new land. They would be there long
enough to build houses, establish family and community
life, and to plant gardens with time to enjoy the produce.
There was no need for 'maintenance only', they could
afford a growth strategy. The prosperity of the land would
be their prosperity as well, and they were to pray for the
peace of Babylon. Anyone who prophesied and incited to
the contrary should be ignored. Yes, there would be a
future in Jerusalem, but not for a long time. God knew
what he was doing; this whole exile was in his hands and it
would not end until his purpose was achieved. That could
not happen before a deep repentance and spiritual hunger
had risen from the people: 'You will seek me and find me
when you seek me with all your heart. I will be found by
you...and will bring you back from captivity' (Jer 29:13–
14). More than this, God's whole attention was with the
exiles. They were not the forsaken ones, as many of them
complained; the forsaken ones were those still in
Jerusalem: 'I will make them like poor figs that are so bad

they cannot be eaten' (Jer 29:17). At all costs the people must acknowledge my letter as the word of God, and turn away from those who offered them contrasting advice.

The letter could have been sound common sense. Any politician with a shrewd mind could realise that Nebuchadnezzar was not about to be toppled, nor was he about to put mercy at the top of his agenda for the exiles. Any counsellor could tell you that the mental anguish of resentment and despair needed lifting into acceptance before the community spirit could find fresh purpose and hope. But I wrote from God. This was his word, explaining his will and offering a different kind of hope; a hope whose sole validity lay in the reliability of the word God speaks and the promise he gives, although it is still a long way from any tangible authentication.

I have many faults, but naivete is not one of them. I knew full well that this was more than a pastoral letter. It was a direct challenge to a pagan outlook. I was claiming that communion with God is independent of both land and Temple. I was setting religion free from all forms of national worship so that a new era could begin in Babylon. In one sense this was not a new idea. The patriarchs had known answered prayers and had exercised their devotions outside their land and its sanctuaries. Elijah saw amazing wonders in a Phoenician town when the son of a widow in Zarephath was restored to life (1 Kings 17:7–24). My point was that the prophets in Babylon were amazed that some remnant of their religion could continue in their exile, and I was insisting that its complete essence and reality could continue there. The total destruction of all externals—Temple, holy city and ritual—could not destroy the fact that God was active in power and able to meet them at every point of their search for him, wherever they were.

My letter was a missile hurled into the midst of a suicidal conspiracy. I timed it with meticulous care. Zedekiah was gathering representatives from local states in order to raise a rebellion against Nebuchadnezzar. They met in Jerusalem for an extravagant banquet and plotted their revolt (Jer 27:3). Of course I realised this would be suicide. Any army captain could judge that for himself.

Military advice was not really my scene, but it was not the point I was making in my letter. I knew that this conspiracy to rebel was a direct onslaught on the word and plan of God. He was taking us into exile, and the period of time would not be cut short by the precipitate action of unbelieving rebels. 'Because you have not listened to my words, I will summon...my servant Nebuchadnezzar' (Jer 25:8–9). I was prepared to devote all my energies to prevent a second suicidal war with Nebuchadnezzar because I dreaded the consequences of such action. I had fanatical opponents around me, not least among the prophets, and Hananiah is a perfect illustration of such opposition. But I must have had some influence because the conspiracy did not materialise at that point and Zedekiah sent Elasah and Gemariah as ambassadors to Nebuchadnezzar; no doubt to assure him of his support and submission. I was able to use the king's ambassadors as my postmen; one of the few laughs I enjoyed at that time (Jer 29:3). My letter was part of a challenge to all such rebellious plans. They were doomed by Nebuchadnezzar, but they were doomed even more by the God whose intention was crystal clear to me. 'Now I will hand all your countries over to my servant Nebuchadnezzar king of Babylon...All nations will serve him and his son and his grandson until the time for his land comes' (Jer 27:6–7). Not really a letter, was it? More a stick of dynamite.

You have to 'go with God' when he's on the move, because he's like a star runner. Once he moves ahead there's no catching him. You have to stay with him all the time. I don't find that any easier than the rest of the people. I have learned the hard way that he counts himself

free to break every mould I make; to ask of me what I
thought should not be asked, and to call for my acceptance
of people and ideas that I had ear-marked for rejection.
Yet, in a broader understanding of God, I have found
freedom and peace.

I called Nebuchadnezzar God's 'servant'

I'll show this to you in another matter connected with my
plea regarding the exile that we 'go with God'. When I
gatecrashed Zedekiah's banquet, assuring the distinguished company present that Nebuchadnezzar's authority over them was ordained of God and therefore
inevitable, I spoke what I believed to be God's word and I
described Nebuchadnezzar as 'my servant' (Jer 27:6; cf
25:9). It was the second time I had used this inflammatory
description. You should have seen Zedekiah and his visit-
ing gang. I too was shocked. This was outrageous talk. I
knew what I was saying and I trembled, but as I knew
God so I travelled the journeys he planned for me.
Nebuchadnezzar in this matter was his 'servant'.

Of course, Nebuchadnezzar had no such consciousness.
He had too many gods to limit himself to one, and his gods
served him! But our God is a sovereign God of history and
of all time. Nothing lies beyond him, and it cannot be too
much for such a faith to reckon that he chooses men as
instruments of his purpose who have no understanding
that their lives are woven into his will.

Nebuchadnezzar was not without his precedent. Isaiah
offered a breathtaking view of Assyria in his own day:
'The Assyrian, the rod of my anger, in whose hand is the
club of my wrath! I send him against a godless nation, I
despatch him against a people who anger me' (Is 10:5–6).
Isaiah portrayed Assyria as executing a judgement on
Israel in the name of Israel's God, but then over-reaching
herself in arrogance and being herself brought to nothing:
'When the Lord has finished all his work against Mount

Zion and Jerusalem, he will say, "I will punish the king of Assyria for the wilful pride of his heart and the haughty look in his eyes" ' (Is 10:12). I expect a similar fate for Nebuchadnezzar because I don't believe he will resist the temptation to extend his ambition beyond God's appointed limits, of which he himself knows and believes nothing. For us, however, one thing is clear: God has appointed Nebuchadnezzar for a task against us; in that he becomes 'my servant', and it will not be for us to frustrate that purpose. My sense of God's intention to work in this way, and my presentation of it, remains starkly simple: 'See, I am setting before you the way of life and the way of death. Whoever stays in this city will die...But, whoever goes out and surrenders to the Babylonians...will live' (Jer 21:8–9).

My own hunch is that one day God will choose another like Nebuchadnezzar. He will give to him a new and daunting title which will startle the people. That man will be his chosen instrument of our freedom and return to Palestine (Is 44:28; 45:1, 13; 48:14). I cannot see in the remote future that we shall as exiles have the power to free ourselves; we shall need a new army, well disposed towards us. It's no more than a hunch, yet I believe there's some specific faith included in my instinct. For what it's worth, I'd watch in the direction of Persia, but we shall see. I doubt in all honesty if it will come in my lifetime, but I pray for the dawn of such a day. God will not fail his word. He may hide, but he does not disappear.

I wore a yoke at a state banquet

I've already mentioned the yoke incident at some length. It amuses me even to think about it, and I've had a lot of private fun at the expense of those who were my victims. It was that situation which was intended to be a vital part of the message 'go with God'. I appeared to Zedekiah and his foreign friends, and I pressed the point on Hananiah, wearing a wooden yoke, and later an iron yoke, in order to demonstrate visibly my total conviction that God was bringing us to the exile as his act of judgement (Jer 27:2; 28:10, 13–14). All resistance to the exile was therefore futile, and all rebellion against Nebuchadnezzar was a direct flouting of God's sure intention. 'If, however, any nation or kingdom will not serve Nebuchadnezzar king of Babylon or bow its neck under his yoke, I will punish that nation with the sword, famine and plague, declares the Lord, until I destroy it by his hand' (Jer 27:8). I was quite specific to Zedekiah our own king. I had a personal word for him: 'Bow your neck under the yoke of the king of Babylon; serve him and his people, and you will live' (Jer 27:12). I was consistent all through this difficult time, with Zedekiah weakly tossed around by every whisper of rebellion and freedom. When rebellion provoked the siege of Jerusalem which led to the final destruction of the city and its Temple, I still pleaded for an acceptance of God's decree in judgement. Only by receiving his sentence upon us could we enter into a clean future. I told Zedekiah plainly, 'This is what the Lord says: I am about to hand this city over to the king of Babylon, and he will burn it down' (Jer 34:2; cf 32:28–29).

I was not the traitor I was accused of being; I was the only true patriot left. Mine were not the words of treason but of truth and faith. I took what I had learned of God and applied it to the nation's life. You cannot do that in any age without agony and courage, but that's why every group and every people needs the genuine prophet more than they can ever know. God was moving relentlessly in a particular direction. When he does that, at any time, you have only one possibility: go with God, or rebel. I'd rather go with God. The short-term view passes away; this is long-term faith.

12

My Message—4

'God Doesn't Judge Worship on Sundays—He Does It All Week'

The rumour spread through Judah like wildfire: 'Jeremiah wants to ban all worship.' It isn't true, but from what I've seen, we must often tempt the Lord to put a stop to all services, if only for a short time. No, the rumour is false, but it springs into life every time a prophet puts his finger on our national and historic abuse of the many means of worship so wonderfully given to us. It's an old argument and most of my predecessors have contributed to it. I believe that we've all been saying the same thing for a very long time, but the notion is still widely held that we want to put a stop to worship. A key part of my message is thus: 'God doesn't judge worship on Sundays—he does it all week.' That will need some explanation, so here goes.

We, of course, worship on our Sabbath, your Saturday, but I know that you worship on Sundays, so I will talk of Sundays in order to make it easy for you to follow my argument.

Amos brought a devastating criticism of the cult of his day: 'I hate, I despise your religious feasts; I cannot stand your assemblies...Away with the noise of your songs!' (Amos 5:21, 23). That was his grasp of God's message to Israel at the time. We must not take those words out of

129

their rightful context. It was the worship as Amos perceived it which had become unacceptable to God. The cult had become mixed with directly immoral elements— sacred prostitution was rampant at the time. The worship of foreign gods and idols was practised alongside the cult of the Lord. But, more than anything else, the worship was offered by people with tainted lives: 'You trample on the poor...You oppress the righteous and take bribes...Father and son use the same girl...In the house of their god they drink wine taken as fines...You have turned justice into poison' (Amos 5:11–12; 2:7–8; 6:12). Amos declared a worship finished even before it started. It was a completely new argument about worship and much more important than those many of you have nowadays. It was not the rejection of all services by Amos, it was a plea for righteous and just people to offer worship: 'Let justice roll on like a river, righteousness like a never-failing stream!' (Amos 5:24).

Hosea took a similar view to Amos. He too saw a cult completely syncretised with the worship of the Canaanite Baal, and he considered the possibility of Israel deprived of all worship in the time of inevitable punishment for the nation: 'For the Israelites will live for many days...without sacrifice or sacred stones, without ephod or idol' (Hos 3:4). Again, the requirement was not for correct services but for acceptable living: 'For I desire mercy, not sacrifice, and acknowledgment of God rather than burnt offerings' (Hos 6:6). It's fascinating, isn't it, to realise that our arguments and tensions which centre on worship are not those which matter to God. His point of view is so different from ours. When he reacts against our worship with the dire threat, 'The Lord will demolish their altars' (Hos 10:2), it's not the form of our liturgy or our regulations concerning the officials allowed to lead worship which have offended him, it's the way we've been living all week. He makes that clear in his accusation, 'Their heart is deceitful, and now they must bear their guilt' (Hos 10:2).

Perhaps we should insist that all future debates about worship reflect issues which are important to God.

Micah is not as well known as many of our prophets, but he could express himself pretty plainly when he felt like it. His contribution to our theme is important. He imagines a worshipper doing some preparation before the service, which is a most inviting thought and worthy of much imitation. 'With what shall I come before the Lord and bow down before the exalted God? Shall I come before him with burnt offerings...? Will the Lord be pleased with thousands of rams?... He has showed you, O man, what is good. And what does the Lord require of you? To act justly and to love mercy and to walk humbly with your God' (Mic 6:6–8). As with Amos and Hosea, Micah gives the clear impression that most of the debate about worship is settled before the day of worship arrives. We've been slow to give the prominence which the Lord assigns to this uncomfortably challenging dimension to our liturgy.

Micah, too, was deeply disturbed that the people found such easy satisfaction in a meticulous daily performance of the ritual. 'Shall I acquit a man with dishonest scales, with a bag of false weights? Her rich men are violent; her people are liars... All men lie in wait to shed blood... the ruler demands gifts, the judge accepts bribes, the powerful dictate what they desire' (Mic 6:11–12; 7:2–3). The Lord judges worship not only by its content but by the daily life of the people and their concern for a society which is fair towards the weak and poor. We prophets burn with this message. As one writer has put it of Micah: 'What is certain is that for him the contemporary cult had no value in Yahweh's eyes' (Johannes Lindblom, *Prophecy in Ancient Israel* [Blackwell: Oxford, 1962]). Many of us agree with Micah.

Joel has a briefer message than many of us, but he expresses well a particular prophetic concern, and that is for a different spirit among the religious officials; the 'clergy' as you would call them. He looks for something to break through the expected words and deeds of the service; a spirit of repentance and pleading with God. This is at one with my conviction about God's view of our lives and our worship. 'Let the priests, who minister before the Lord, weep between the temple porch and the altar. Let them say, "Spare your people, O Lord...."'... "Rend your heart and not your garments...return to me with all your heart, with fasting and weeping and mourning" ' (Joel 2:17, 13, 12).

I've wanted to be a prophet taking you on a conducted tour of the prophets in order for you to catch this major theme which has gripped all of us. We have been open to the charge that we were bringing the entire cult to an end, as if people would no longer gather to worship their God. That's obviously ridiculous, and we have written too much about right worship and the joy and purity of the presence of God for the conclusion to be drawn that we don't want services. But we are sure of what God wants, and it isn't tainted lives which negate an act of worship even before the day of the service dawns.

I can't show you some of my own teaching on this matter before I've ended the tour with a visit to Isaiah. His attitude may be slightly more complicated than his predecessors', but his basic convictions are no different from theirs. He judges the cultic feasts to be intolerable to the Lord, although his reasons are not fully clear. He felt deeply about this, and he's into it in his first chapter. No time waster was Isaiah. ' "The multitude of your sacrifices—what are they to me?" says the Lord' (Is 1:11). Ceremonial rules demanded ritual purity, but he looked for ethical and moral purity even before the ceremonial regulations were considered. There are neither short-cuts nor by-passes with God. Isaiah's demand is again for social righteousness or for a ban on worship. He makes it as simple as that. We have muddied the waters. We do find in Isaiah a condemnation of sacrifices, sacred festival and prayers, but for a good reason: 'Your hands are full of blood' (Is 1:15). Worship had come to be an expression of defiant spirits, not of devoted lives.

Isaiah loved worship. He was called to be a prophet in the middle of a service in the Temple. He heard the usual cultic music: 'Holy, holy, holy' (Is 6:3). His lips were made clean by a red-hot stone from the incense altar. He later looked to the great singing of the cultic feasts and the procession accompanied by music: 'And you will sing as on the night you celebrate a holy festival' (Is 30:29). Isaiah's thrill at the great acts of worship offered in faith had not blinded him to the spirit the Lord requires of those who draw near to him. Perhaps that is the greatness of this man. He was never blind to those things which seemed to have covered the eyes of the nation: 'Stop bringing meaningless offerings! Your incense is detestable to me... Your New Moon festivals and your appointed feasts my soul hates... I am weary of bearing them' (Is 1:13–14). God is not weary of our worship. Only of unacceptable worship whose quality he judges seven days a week, through our daily lives. 'Seek justice, encourage the oppressed. Defend the cause of the fatherless, plead the case of the widow' (Is 1:17). *Then* come to church!

I fully realise that this is a hobby-horse of mine, and I'm treating it at length. But it's a hobby-horse of the Lord as well, and we need to ride *his* horses not our own. We have seen sweeping reforms from Josiah, but what lasting difference have they made? Before Josiah we had the very teaching of the prophets which I've set in front of you. How did we blow it? I quickly realised that Josiah's reform had not penetrated to the depths. It had not touched the essential spiritual outlook of the people. The Lord wants repentance, moral reform and the abolition of all cultic usages which are alien to true religion. In other words, the Lord wants what the earlier prophets had very clearly proclaimed. In their own distinctive ways they have been saying what I'm now saying: 'God doesn't judge worship only on Sundays, he does it all week.'

I long for a living act of worship; for a people as prepared as they expect their professionals to be; for freedom and order in active balance and occasional tension; for exuberant praise alongside respectful awe. I am not the only one who can name unbelievers drawn to God by the intensity, power and reality of a worshipping community meeting in transparent sincerity. I don't accept any more than you do that one piped instrument can be a valid substitute for our rich scriptural heritage of musical instruments. I do bring, however, a prophetic insistence that God's final accent is somewhere else. He stresses a variety of essential responses which make worship valid or invalid. They are utterly in line with those prophets who have preceded me, and I bring them to your attention to support the thesis of my message. You'll find echoes of each of them in my lesser-known contemporary Zephaniah. He spoke out in the reign of Josiah. Whether or not I influenced him, I do not know; but judge for yourselves the extent to which we are at one in this matter of worship and life.

You cannot worship alongside injustice

I threw down the gauntlet on all sides in my demand for justice. I challenged the various kings whose misfortune it was to be contemporary with me. In one passage I have recorded a challenge for each of Zedekiah's three immediate predecessors. Jehoahaz, 'Shallum' to some, only lasted three months after the death of his father, Josiah. That was long enough for him to show his true colours, and I managed to confront him even in that short space of time. I exposed his record: 'Woe to him who builds his palace by unrighteousness, his upper rooms by injustice, making his countrymen work for nothing, not paying them for their labour' (Jer 22:13). Then I put before him the fine example of his father: ' "He defended the cause of the poor and needy...Is that not what it means to know me?" declares the Lord. "But your eyes and your heart are set only on dishonest gain, on shedding innocent blood and on oppression and extortion" ' (Jer 22:16–17).

Several years later I had a message for Zedekiah and his generation: 'O house of David, this is what the Lord says: "Administer justice every morning; rescue from the hand of his oppressor the one who has been robbed" ' (Jer 21:12). My general word to kings followed this theme. I was prepared to be monotonous if that was necessary to press home the Lord's requirement: 'Do what is just and right. Rescue from the hand of his oppressor the one who has been robbed. Do no wrong or violence to the alien, the fatherless or the widow, and do not shed innocent blood in this place...If you do not obey these commands, declares the Lord, I swear by myself that this palace will become a ruin' (Jer 22:3–5).

The call went wider than to the palace. The city itself, Jerusalem, bore the brunt of my anger and my passion. 'As a well pours out its water, so she pours out her wickedness. Violence and destruction resound in her; her sickness and wounds are ever before me. Take warning, O Jerusalem' (Jer 6:7–8). As I viewed life in the city, I felt you'd be hard pressed to find anyone living close to the demands of holiness: 'Go up and down the streets of Jerusalem, look around and consider, search through her squares. If you can find but one person who deals honestly and seeks the truth, I will forgive this city' (Jer 5:1). Even Abraham was content to find only ten righteous people in Sodom, and I was stuck for one in Jerusalem!

I would leave no stone unturned to present my message and to be sure that no one had escaped me. My Temple address did take my life in my hands, but it seemed vital to bring this word to the very precinct of worship itself: 'Do not trust in deceptive words and say, "This is the temple of the Lord, the temple of the Lord, the temple of the

Lord" ' (Jer 7:4). I was not wanting to mock their songs, but their lives had emptied the songs of all meaning. This was sermon time, not worship time. 'If you really change your ways and your actions and deal with each other justly, if you do not oppress the alien, the fatherless or the widow and do not shed innocent blood in this place...But look, you are trusting in deceptive words that are worthless...Will you steal and murder, commit adultery and perjury, burn incense to Baal and follow other gods you have not known, and then come and stand before me in this house, which bears my Name?' (Jer 7:5–10). God was affronted and threatening: 'I have been watching! declares the Lord' (Jer 7:11). That brought back to me his promise at my call: 'I am watching to see that my word is fulfilled' (Jer 1:12). I was deep in the character of God. I was mining, and bringing gold to the surface. ' "Let him who boasts boast about this: that he understands and knows me, that I am the Lord, who exercises kindness, justice and righteousness on earth, for in these I delight," declares the Lord' (Jer 9:24).

Zephaniah saw it my way: 'Woe to the city of oppressors, rebellious and defiled...she does not draw near to her God...every new day he does not fail, yet the unrighteous know no shame' (Zeph 3:1–2, 5). This was no peculiarity of Jeremiah; this was the voice of the prophets of the Lord.

You cannot worship alongside disobedience

I'm not sure how much evidence and illustration to give you in these descriptions of my important emphases. I'm trying to draw as complete a picture as possible, allowing my words to speak for themselves. I can easily use one particular example when I speak of obedience as an indispensable partner of those who would worship God. Obviously, there will be so much which I have to omit.

The Recabites are not very well known, and they are

probably more familiar through me than through anyone else. Way back in the time of Elisha, Jehu launched a terrible massacre of Ahab's family and all the officials of the Baal cult which Jezebel had introduced among us. Jehu took with him Jonadab, son of Recab. Jonadab was to witness Jehu's murderous 'zeal for the Lord' (2 Kings 10:16). Presumably, Jonadab's own uncompromising faith must have been known to all. Normally the Recabites lived as wanderers, unattached to the land. At the same time, they were fervent in their worship of the Lord. They represented the nomadic ideal of the prophets, serving as a living condemnation of the affluence of city life. They lived far from urban civilisation and only came to the city in exceptional circumstances. I had a brief encounter with them which serves as a classic example of the significance of obedience for worship. It was more than an illustration; it was an example of prophetic symbolism.

I invited some of the Recabites to the Temple and offered them a drink of wine (Jer 35:5). They refused adamantly, reminding me of the instruction of Jonadab: 'Neither you nor your descendants must ever drink wine. Also you must never build houses, sow seed or plant vineyards...but must always live in tents' (Jer 35:6–7). Their faithful loyalty to the command of their ancestor became for me a vivid lesson to those Jews who would no longer obey the word of the Lord: ' "Will you not learn a lesson and obey my words?" declares the Lord' (Jer 35:13). 'I have spoken to you again and again, yet you have not obeyed me. Jonadab son of Recab ordered his sons not to drink wine and this command has been kept' (Jer 35:14). In one sense the Recabites were a group of extremists, but they made vows to the Lord and kept them. Worship is not worship until obedience is its companion, and I used this incident as a telling reminder to the people.

Naturally, I nailed disobedience on many occasions. I was sorely provoked by those who violated the Sabbath:

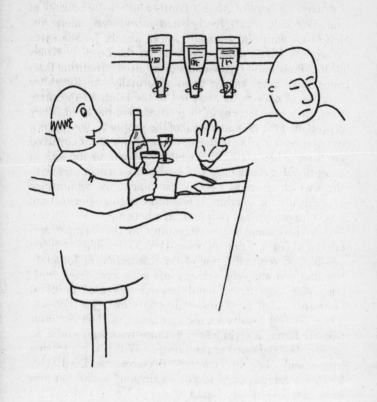

'This is what the Lord says…keep the Sabbath day holy…. Yet they did not listen or pay attention' (Jer 17:21–23). I confronted Jehoiakim, another of Josiah's sons, and exposed his sin: 'This has been your way from your youth; you have not obeyed me' (Jer 22:21). I captured our history in a sentence or two: 'You have behaved more wickedly than your fathers. See how each of you is following the stubbornness of his evil heart instead of obeying me' (Jer 16:12). Again, I am not a lone voice. My contemporary Zephaniah is with me as he denounces Jerusalem: 'She obeys no-one, she accepts no correction…she does not draw near to her God.' 'I will bring distress on the people…because they have sinned against the Lord' (Zeph 3:12; 1:17).

You cannot worship alongside dishonesty

Here is a golden thread which holds together all revelation of God—he is a God of truth. If ever the Lord reveals himself in human form, the commitment to truth will be paramount in that person (eg Jn 8:45, 51; 14:6). Lies therefore are detestable to him. Liars are unacceptable as worshippers, and that makes life difficult for our generation. As soon as a society begins to decay, truth becomes dispensable, and we find that lying and injustice go hand in hand. 'Like a partridge that hatches eggs it did not lay is the man who gains riches by unjust means' (Jer 17:11). It sounds like one of the proverbs, doesn't it? But it's one of my sayings.

I came down hard on dishonesty, whatever its form. I've already told you about the Lord's vain search for one in Jerusalem 'who deals honestly and seeks the truth' (Jer 5:1). People were swearing by the Lord's name, and swearing falsely. I don't see why they can't tell the truth without needing oaths at all, because I'm sure that's the only reason why oaths are allowed—we have to find a way of guaranteeing truth. God judges worship whenever people lie, and he rejects it. When people lie to each other, they destroy the vital foundations of trust and friendship: 'Truth has perished; it has vanished from their lips' (Jer 7:28). 'They have taught their tongues to lie...Beware of your friends; do not trust your brothers' (Jer 9:5, 4). It is then a short step to allow these standards to infiltrate worship, missing the call of God: 'They have lied about the Lord; they said, "He will do nothing" ' (Jer 5:12). God's response is swift and sharp: 'Because the people have spoken these words...O house of Israel...I am bringing a distant nation against you' (Jer 5:14–15). Clearly, God judges liars. Zephaniah looked to a better day when judgement had worked its way through the nation and its lessons had been absorbed: 'The remnant of Israel will do no wrong; they will speak no lies, nor will deceit be found in their mouths' (Zeph 3:13).

I hope I've made my point. There are more examples which I could give, but they will simply add to the argument I've been following so far. I have taken a similar line with regard to purity and repentance. The more you read of my work the more you will recognise my ruthless determination to preserve a pure ritual and to press for a repentant people: ' "Although you wash yourself with soda and use an abundance of soap, the stain of your guilt is still before me," declares the Sovereign Lord. "How can you say, 'I am not defiled; I have not run after the Baals'?" (Jer 2:22–23). No-one repents of his wickedness...my people do not know the requirements of the Lord' (Jer 8:6–7). I tried to express national repentance for myself, as a sort of priest for the entire country: 'O Lord, we acknowledge our wickedness and the guilt of our fathers; we have sinned against you' (Jer 14:20). Zephaniah felt as deeply as I did. He condemned those who bowed down to the Queen of Heaven in their sordid rooftop rites: 'Those who bow down on the housetops to worship the starry host...those who turn back from following the Lord and neither seek the Lord nor enquire of him' (Zeph 1:5–6). He too looked for that quietness of spirit which indicates true penitence before God: 'Seek the Lord, all you humble of the land…seek righteousness, seek humility' (Zeph 2:3).

There is one more part of my theme (God doesn't judge worship on Sundays, he does it all week) which I want to mention. I see this as very relevant to the clergy. I waged a running battle with corrupt officials of the cult of the Lord. The rot came from the top and spread down through the whole body of worship. I don't know if I sparked Ezekiel into his marvellous picture of God as the takeover Shepherd of the people (Ezek 34:11ff), but I do see these men— prophets, priests and elders—as shepherds living in falsehood and apathy: ' "Woe to the shepherds who are destroying and scattering the sheep of my pasture!" declares the Lord' (Jer 23:1). God had seen their wickedness in the Temple itself, and I don't see how they could expect valid worship when the Lord was committed to staying away. Their corruption knew no bounds, and I waged war on their sin and their heartlessness: 'Prophets and priests alike, all practise deceit…among the prophets of Jerusalem I have seen something horrible: They commit adultery and live a lie' (Jer 8:10; 23:14). There is much more to be said, but my point has been made. You cannot worship alongside a corrupt clergy, but you can certainly worship without any clergy at all. Let them be warned. Once more Zephaniah speaks from Jerusalem: 'Her prophets are arrogant…Her priests profane the sanctuary…The Lord within her is righteous' (Zeph 3:4–5).

I believe the door of worship remains open to those who walk closely with God. He takes delight in those who come worthily to him: 'Blessed is the man who trusts in the Lord, whose confidence is in him…I the Lord search the heart and examine the mind…a glorious throne, exalted from the beginning is the place of our sanctuary' (Jer 7:10, 12). From such personal devotion and faith rises the beauty and power of worship, and we are allowed to be part of it. When we come before him we bring every day, every activity, every word and every thought. It's daunting, but it's wonderful.

13

My Message—5

'There Is Hope Yet'

The better you know God, the nearer he brings you to his heart which beats with mercy as well as power. He has revealed to me a terrible but irrevocable judgement on our nation, but that is not his final word. Judgement will be followed by renewal; doom by promise. Any grasp I have of the future rises not from my vivid imagination—for my portrait of the future has been described as 'disappointingly sober' (Gerhard Von Rad, *Old Testament Theology*, Vol 2 [SCM: London, 1975]), nor does it progress from the transformation of a pessimist into an optimist. The future I see arrives solely from the God I know. I believe that 'there is hope yet', and my message is impregnated with hope in a number of ways which I want to set before you now. Watch carefully as I write, for there are plenty who reduce Jeremiah's hope to a mere shadow, missing the richness of all that God has revealed to me. The one who was called 'to uproot and tear down, to destroy and overthrow', was also called 'to build and to plant' (Jer 1:10).

The New Covenant

The covenant idea was always for me a valid expression of

our religious bond with God. God is a God of covenant, pledging himself to men, sealing that pledge in conscious covenant, and requiring allegiance and obedience from those bound to him in this vital relationship. The covenant is one of the unique glories of Israel's faith, and one day it will be our gift to all the nations. Traditionally, a covenant would set conditions for Israel—usually of exclusive allegiance and total obedience to the Lord, especially to his will as expressed in the law. The Lord, for his part, would make promises to Israel, usually to treat her as his chosen people and to secure that choice in their possession of the land of Canaan.

I revel in such a God, and I'm not the first to expose a grotesque form of spiritual adultery in the frivolous way we have spurned our covenant obligations for a religion and ritual which appear to be more attractive. 'They have forsaken the covenant of the Lord their God and have worshipped and served other gods...the land is full of adulterers' (Jer 22:9; 23:10); ' "They broke my covenant, though I was a husband to them," declares the Lord' (Jer 31:32).

I have used the covenant idea very fully in my message, not because I am locked into something formal and rigid, but because it represents the fundamental and mutual commitment between God and Israel. I spoke often of the covenant Moses made with God at Sinai: 'Cursed is the man who does not obey the terms of this covenant—the terms I commanded your forefathers when I brought them out of Egypt' (Jer 11:3–4). I said, 'Obey me and do everything I command you, and you will be my people, and I will be your God' (Jer 11:4). I viewed Josiah's reforms as the renewal of the covenant, and I accused Zedekiah of violating the covenant when he refused to fulfil its obligations to free all slaves after six years of slavery. 'But now you have turned around and profaned my name; each of you has taken back the male and female slaves you had set free to go where they wished. You have forced them to become your slaves again' (Jer 34:16).

I described God's agreement with King David as a covenant—'my covenant with David my servant' (Jer 33:21)—and foresaw the possibility of that covenant being terminated—'My covenant...can be broken and David will no longer have a descendant to reign on his throne' (Jer 33:21). I understood my own role as the Lord's messenger as one which required me to speak for him and to make a continual proclamation of his covenant demands.

In my turmoil and anger, I caught sight of a New Covenant, and I wrote down what was shown to me. There will always be those who see these parts of my message as incompatible with my personal despair and message of judgement. But that judgement was never to be final, and my understanding of God demanded a new and better future once judgement had been fulfilled. This New Covenant would be a new relationship between God and Israel. It would include the whole nation, not one of two divided kingdoms. I was prepared for this by a real-isation of God's heart for Ephraim, the northern kingdom, to which I had an ancestral affinity. 'At that time...I will be the God of all the clans of Israel, and they will be my people...I will build you up again and you will be rebuilt, O Virgin Israel...I have surely heard Ephraim's moan-ing: "...Restore me, and I will return, because you are the Lord my God. After I strayed, I repented...." Is not Ephraim my dear son, the child in whom I delight?... Therefore my heart yearns for him; I have great compas-sion for him...The time is coming...when I will make a new covenant with the house of Israel and with the house of Judah' (Jer 31:1, 4, 18–20, 31). Hosea had stood at the end of the northern kingdom and I was now standing on the edge of the precipice over which the southern kingdom would plunge. As I stood there, I proclaimed a new begin-ning for both Israel and Judah. God seemed to challenge me: 'Is your heart large enough to welcome what I will do?'

We would recognise this covenant, despite its newness, because it would be an obvious but wonderful new edition of the former, and it would fulfil the original intention of Moses' covenant at Sinai. Previous failure would be put behind us. No more would we hear those awful words, 'A most horrible thing has been done by Virgin Israel' (Jer 18:13). The specific formula of the covenant would ring again: 'I will be their God, and they will be my people' (Jer 31:33). These words gripped me throughout my life. They were the great prize we were losing, and now they were being restored to us in a free act of God's grace. I had been banned from dancing with others, but I did my own private jig when this covenant promise was given to me. I have a hunch that God has nothing greater to say than this, if it is rightly believed and fathomed: 'I will be their God, and they will be my people' (Jer 31:33). The words would not be enlarged, rather they would be more fully realised in the new future coming to us.

The covenant would be new as 'forgiveness'

'For I will forgive their wickedness and will remember their sins no more' (Jer 31:34). To me the miracle of forgiveness lies in learning how to give and to receive this 'remembering sins no more'. I can remember wrongs against me with no difficulty at all. If God is willing to blot our sin from his memory, then we shall indeed be in a new age. If only we can extend his grace and offer this to each other. If only I can set a living example. I think I see that there will be no other way to establish and to maintain the relationship with God which has to be real, but also lasting and inward. If he does not forgive, freely and utterly, we shall stumble on from disobedience to despair, but if he is willing to forgive where we can claim nothing, then we shall have a life and an experience which will burst every restriction of Israel.

The covenant would be new as 'inwardness'

'I will put my law in their minds and write it on their hearts' (Jer 31:33). Of course the law would move outward with dynamic effect, but only because of its inner source and reality. We had plunged into national and spiritual disintegration because we had settled easily for an outward performance whose sole requirement was correct ritual. I glimpsed the possibility of a new work of God which would claim everything that a person is, leading him or her to see his or her thoughts and motives as exposed to God, however skilfully they may be hidden from others. I recognised that the New Covenant would not annul the former, but would bring it to its ideal realisation, demonstrating perfectly to a fickle people the consistency of God.

The covenant would be new as 'personal'

'They will all know me, from the least of them to the greatest' (Jer 31:34). The Old Covenant had been written on stone: 'When the Lord finished speaking to Moses on Mount Sinai, he gave him the two tablets of the Testimony, the tablets of stone inscribed by the finger of God' (Ex 31:18). It had been put into a book: '[Moses] took the Book of the Covenant and read it to the people' (Ex 24:7). For as long as it was external it would fail to win the allegiance of the people. Now the Lord would bring the necessary change in each person, writing his will on their hearts, reaching their minds and their wills. I would not want this to be called 'individualism', although I admit this has happened frequently in analyses of my teaching. I was trying to burrow into the depths of personal faith, deeper than any of my predecessors, in order to pave the way for a new community of God based on personal allegiance and decision. When the social order was shattered I saw that a person could trust God with his entire being and I found this to be explicit in the New Covenant.

Such a person would belong fully to the covenant community, and I believe I made this clear by restating the great covenant promise: 'I will be their God, and they will be my people' (Jer 31:33). No intermediaries would be needed to achieve this reality of personal faith. In the past, men like Moses, prophets, teachers, priests had all played their crucial part in instructing people to know the Lord. Now we could look forward to a New Covenant: 'No longer will a man teach his neighbour, or a man his brother, saying, "Know the Lord," because they will all know me, from the least of them to the greatest' (Jer 31:34).

This New Covenant would have about it an unfailing quality, and I used extreme possibilities to make my point: ' "Only if the heavens above can be measured and the foundations of the earth below be searched out will I reject all the descendants of Israel because of all they have done," declares the Lord' (Jer 31:37).

The coming of this New Covenant surpasses anything we can yet imagine. It will possess an eternal quality which defies our grasp of its human realisation. 'I will make an everlasting covenant with them: I will never stop doing good to them, and I will inspire them to fear me, so that they will never turn away from me. I will rejoice in doing them good and will assuredly plant them in this land with all my heart and soul' (Jer 32:40–41). I believe that a completely new teaching and experience of what we at present call 'the Spirit of the Lord' will be an essential dimension of the arrival of the day of the New Covenant. More than that I cannot see, but I am peering as intently as I can. The day will be a glorious day and I detect stirrings in other prophets before me who have also longed for a fuller expression of our knowledge of God. I speak of a New Covenant, and in that I express some of my conviction that 'there is hope yet'. Joel, to give but one example, looked to a time when 'I will pour out my Spirit on all people. Your sons and daughters will prophesy, your old men will dream dreams, your young men will see visions.... And everyone who calls on the name of the Lord will be saved' (Joel 2:28, 32). They'll have to let women speak in the days of the New Covenant, so that they can give the prophecy given to them!

The field I bought

I put my money where my mouth was. In a day of financial collapse I invested in a field (Jer 32:9). It was virtually a symbolic action—'prophetic symbolism'—but I've saved this example until now in order to convince you of my considerable faith for a future with God. There is hope yet. Those who fear God need not fear putting their money where their mouth is. This is no gamble, for they will be vindicated.

It was a time of appalling deprivation and humiliation. 'With their own hands compassionate women have cooked their own children, who became their food when my people were destroyed' (Lam 4:10). 'Death has climbed in through our windows and has entered our fortresses' (Jer 9:21). I was languishing in prison, confined to the guard's courtyard in the royal palace. Nebuchadnezzar was besieging Jerusalem because of the suicidally stupid rebellion of Zedekiah. Nebuchadnezzar simply arrived at Jerusalem, settled outside it and built siege works to close up the city. Famine, disease and low morale overwhelmed us, and the end was only a matter of time. We could expect no mercy from our enemy, and none was shown when the time came (2 Kings 24:10—25:21). Zedekiah had confined me out of sheer exasperation at my insistence that we submit to Babylon's rule and accept the exile. I, for my part, had consistently warned against the very rebellion which was now destroying a people—God's chosen people.

In the middle of all this God spoke to me. Hanamel, one of my cousins from Anathoth, came to me to offer me the purchase of his field there (Jer 32:8). He was a cunning little relative. He knew full well that I had a family duty to buy the field, but in fact it was worth very little, not least because we could not expect to make any use of it for years because of the inevitably long exile. He was trying to hang me by my own words. You probably know about the duties which a nearest relative has to carry out. Boaz married Ruth out of his responsibility to be her 'redeemer' as her nearest relative (Ruth 4:13). I was called to buy this field under the same set of responsibilities. My family knew where to come when they wanted some ready cash. It's like all panic—if you sleep on it for a night it becomes a non-event and God works wonderfully through it. God spoke to me, and I agreed with Hanamel to buy his wretched, grubby field. Someone has asked, in the latest Jewish joke, 'Why did God make the Gentiles?' I gather that the answer is, 'Well, someone had to pay retail.' I can tell you that I paid through the nose for Hanamel's piece of land, seventeen shekels of silver (Jer 32:9). It was worth it for the object lesson to Israel, otherwise it was a rip-off.

I signed the purchase deed, properly in front of witnesses, and I weighed out the money. I handed over all the paperwork to Baruch (that's what secretaries and personal assistants are for) and I ensured that a good number of people saw the entire transaction. I asked Baruch to put all the documents into a clay jar as a sign that I wanted them kept for a very long time. The crowd was fascinated, imagining that Jeremiah had at last flipped his lid, but he knew exactly what he was doing. This was a symbolic action, and its message was to be loud and clear: 'Houses, fields and vineyards will again be bought in this land' (Jer 32:15).

I'd had my own problems with this one. It was another of my arguments with the Lord. I wonder at times why he hasn't hung up on me, but I praise him for his patience. My query was simple: 'Though the city will be handed over to the Babylonians, you, O Sovereign Lord, say to

me, "Buy the field with silver and have the transaction witnessed" ' (Jer 32:25). He hung me on my own words, as Hanamel had attempted, only he was more effective. I had recently launched my own worship song: 'Ah, Sovereign Lord, you have made the heavens and the earth by your great power and outstretched arm. Nothing is too hard for you' (Jer 32:17). At least I know that our worship songs get through to the Lord, because his response to my query cut me right down to size: 'I am the Lord, the God of all mankind. Is anything too hard for me?' (Jer 32:27). He paraded his plan of judgement before me, giving a devastating recitation of the sin of Judah, but then the promise followed the judgement: 'I will bring them back to this place and let them live in safety. They will be my people, and I will be their God...Once more fields will be bought in this land of which you say, "It is a desolate waste, without men or animals, for it has been handed over to the Babylonians." Fields will be bought for silver, and deeds will be signed, sealed and witnessed' (Jer 32:37–38, 43–44). I bought Hanamel's field in Anathoth as a sign of my total commitment to that time, whose only likelihood was that God had declared its eventual coming. There is hope yet and I put my money where my mouth was.

The branch of David

When I looked back, I drew on the tradition of the Exodus and Sinai: 'I remember the devotion of your youth...what fault did your fathers find in me?... They did not ask, "Where is the Lord who brought us up out of Egypt...?" ' (Jer 2:2, 5–6). When I looked forward I did the same, in terms of a New Covenant: 'It will not be like the covenant I made with their forefathers when I took them by the hand to lead them out of Egypt' (Jer 31:32). This, however, in no way exhausted my concept of the future and I drew on the rich traditions of our messianic hopes which were attached to the person of David. I did not employ the grandeur and power of Isaiah's visions (Is 9:2–7; 11:1–10) but I rested in calm acknowledgement of the existing categories of expectation (Jer 23:5–6; 33:15–26). I was happy to use the persistent central features of our messianic hopes. There is hope yet, and a clear strand of our Jewish view for the future sees it in a Messiah who will be the ideal King, ruling through his unique relationship with the Lord, coming from the house and line of David, and exercising that rule in wisdom and righteousness.

In a reaction against the useless spiritual shepherds of our day, 'Woe to the shepherds who are destroying and scattering the sheep of my pasture!' (Jer 23:1), I looked to a righteous branch being raised up for David. 'I will raise up to David a righteous Branch, a King who will reign wisely and do what is just and right in the land' (Jer 23:5). I didn't need colourful or bizarre descriptions merely to avoid the charge of dullness or repetition. These were traditional concepts I was using, and they fitted what I had to say. The King to come would be a shepherd, with special importance in his throne names, and righteousness and wisdom as the hallmarks of his rule. I saw no outward splendour, rather calm in a new life we would experience in Canaan.

In another passage I foresaw a further aspect of the coming of the Anointed One: 'I will bring him near and he will come close to me' (Jer 30:21). The idea of 'drawing near' is a technical term of the priesthood as I know perfectly well from my family background. But my real aim was to depict a particular court privilege of direct access to the king. My view of the Anointed One was that he would be the Lord's representative on earth, in intimate fellowship with him. The Anointed One would have free access to the Lord, dealing directly with him. This access would be reserved for the Anointed One, and no one else would dare to 'devote himself to be close to me' (Jer 30:21). I drew this expression, 'devote himself to be close to me', from the sphere of the lawcourt, where it refers to the giving of a security. The access to the Lord which I held out to the Anointed One required his willingness to offer up his life—'devoting himself'. I never forgot the belief of our early years that anyone who drew near to the Lord to 'see' him would die (Ex 33:20). Access to God, entry to his presence, remains for us an aweful possibility. I was putting a tough question which only the Anointed One could answer positively: 'Who will devote himself to be close to me?' I wanted to break through nationalistic limitations in my anxiety to present a deeply personal experience of religion. Here I felt I had discovered a way forward. I could use traditional ideas in our Jewish expectation, but I could also move further into direct communion with God as the basis of restored life beyond the exile. I wanted to demonstrate that we could know God fully, even in Babylonian exile, despite the exclusion there of the Messiah. At the same time, I looked beyond the exile to a new day where one from David's line would rule in righteousness and wisdom as God's representative among men.

I looked carefully, and I saw life beyond the exile. The vision is still with me, although I wonder at times if I shall need the persistence of Abraham to cling to this promise as a genuine possibility. I am not sustained by our circumstances. They afford us no grounds for hope. I am kept by the promise of God. It stays alive in me through my certainty that the exile is a punishment which one day will be exhausted and God will do a new work among us. It comes back to me in my dreams. In one dream I saw the return from captivity. The people were in their towns of Judah; God's blessing was upon Zion; the farmers were on the move with their flocks. I heard God say, 'I will refresh the weary and satisfy the faint' (Jer 31:25). I recognised those words as words typical of prophetic hopes for a new day. Then my dream ended. 'At this I awoke and looked around. My sleep had been pleasant to me' (Jer 31:26). I became bold, and once more I spelled out the life we shall know, whether in my lifetime or not I don't know. I doubt it, but the day will come to our people. ' "The days are coming," declares the Lord, "when I will plant the house of Israel and the house of Judah with the offspring of men and of animals...I will watch over them to build and to plant" ' (Jer 31:27–28).

All that my critics seem to hear now is my insistence on the judgement, deserved judgement, of exile. One day, for my words are written down, they will read what I have said, and I shall be acknowledged at last as a true prophet. For I see a return from exile and a new life, and that return will come. 'There is hope yet,' and I have lived to declare it.

I Am Joseph

by Alan Pain

You've heard all about his amazing Technicolour dreamcoat.

Now meet the star behind the stripes.

From slave in Egypt to Pharaoh's right-hand man, Joseph's meteoric rise to fame charts a story of family intrigue, murderous jealousy, sexual drama, incredible rescue, prophetic dreams, and final reconciliation.

'An imaginative and challenging first-person presentation and application of the exciting biblical adventure of Joseph.'

DAVID COHEN
General Director, Scripture Union

'Shows that yesterday's heroes have genuine relevance to today's generation. Packed with plenty of spiritual sting in the tail.'

CLIVE CALVER
General Director, Evangelical Alliance

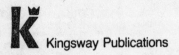

Kingsway Publications

God Meant it for Good

by R. T. Kendall

'When I came to Westminster Chapel at the age of forty-one I thought, "Surely I am ready now." But in a matter of months I could sense that I was still in the process of being prepared. That was most humbling indeed. There is a kind of preparation that cannot be found in university . . . it is that which God sovereignly ordains for a specific purpose and which drives us to our knees and to tears.'

R. T. Kendall, Minister of Westminster Chapel in the heart of London, here reveals from the biblical story of Joseph how God works for those he loves.

Here we see the young and impetuous Joseph develop through sometimes painful and trying experience into a mature man willing to leave his own vindication with God. As we see Joseph learn what it means to forgive others totally—from the heart—we discover some of the wonderful ways in which our patient, loving God prepares us for his service.

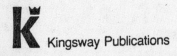

Kingsway Publications

30 Days To Understanding The Bible

by Max E. Anders

'If you'll give me fifteen minutes a day for thirty days, I'll give you an understanding of the Bible.'

A mature grasp of the Bible will take a lifetime. But this remarkable book will set you on the road. Max Anders sets out for you:

- The major events
- The key people
- The significant locations
- The essential chronology
- The basic doctrines

For those who are just starting out in their Christian faith—and for those many Christians who have never really got to grips with their Bible—this book is an invaluable tool: a month that will lay the foundations for a proper understanding.

A pastor and teacher, **DR MAX E. ANDERS** is a graduate of Dallas Theological Seminary and Western Conservative Baptist Seminary. For many years he has contributed to *Walk Through the Bible*.

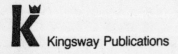

Kingsway Publications